Where t...... a Will...

Introduction

Destiny is not something in which I believe. I have always taken with a pinch of salt the views of those who make such assertions, never believing that things are "meant to be" or "happen for a reason". Having studied Philosophy and Theology, it is difficult to square that notion with any understanding of why suffering occurs or nasty things happen. How could we operate as ourselves in a world pre-programmed; our lives set in stone. Surely it is better to have fully lived, being ourselves within the world around us, whatever life (not destiny) throws our way.

Yet the story of "Will" is so surprising that its ultimate conclusion has led many to remark that destiny played its part. Perhaps...perhaps not. Whatever the mysterious workings of this universe, it is clear that sometimes, just sometimes, failing to take 'no' for an answer, combined with sheer determination, a sprinkling of luck as well as being in the right place at the right time, can lead to life changing conclusions.

Animals are often not given enough air time or media attention. The abuses and neglect so many endure remains hidden behind closed doors, acknowledged only by those who campaign vigorously on their behalf. It is very difficult to get legislation passed to defend animals as often the laws are vague with many exceptions. Too frequently it takes years for change to be enacted. Many people are shocked by the realities when it is drawn to their attention and it would be good for right to prevail. Often people who fight for animals are not given a fair press. However, we fight for animals because we recognise each creature's unique individuality and the mass importance of animal welfare as a whole. If every human being adhered to this, the animal welfare movement would not even be necessary.

However, while one animal is in need, there will be those who remain steadfastly committed to helping them, whatever others might say. Somebody has to.

Chapter One

"I'm not having a dog"

Will's story starts six years before we would become aware of his existence. My mum, Val, and I had started volunteering at a greyhound rescue centre, about thirty minutes drive from our house.

I had wanted a dog for years. I remember when I was aged about thirteen, sitting in a French lesson. The class had been asked what they 'needed'. My answer had been "un chien". Needless to say, I received a withering look from the teacher! My mother was about to give me the same look! We had several animals at home including my first ever pet, a very special cat called Pudding. There were also four other stray cats that had arrived on our doorstep.

It is clear that any animal in distress gravitates to those who want (or who are there) to help them! Any animal in need seemed to be directed to the Clark household. There must be a 999 service for animals which gives out directions to our home! We have had injured foxes, desperate ducks, marooned swans and even a lost Polish homing pigeon land in our porch seeking refuge.

The presence of five cats and the prospect of other waifs and strays systematically turning up seeking sanctuary prompted an outraged response when I requested we add to the menagerie by also getting a dog.

"No way, I have enough to do" was the abrupt answer from my mum, despite my protestations that any canine addition would be solely my responsibility.

I was at university, studying from home; I was not abandoning her to a lifetime of puppy training while I swanned off on my travels around the world. Why could I not have a dog?

We reached an uneasy compromise. We lived near to a Greyhound stadium and my support for animal welfare organisations had highlighted the plight of ex-racing greyhounds and the desperate and ongoing need for homes following the end of their racing careers. Thousands of greyhounds retire from racing each year in the UK and many more in the Republic of Ireland. Many are under five years old and some as young as eighteen months old. I discovered that the local stadium had a rehoming centre attached to it which was always looking out for volunteer walkers. If I couldn't have a dog at home, walking homeless hounds would be the next best thing. It took some persuasion and further pressure to force mum through the gates, but gradually the dogs won her round and, with the promise that we would not be taking any home, we quickly became regulars at the kennels.

It soon became clear that greyhounds are wonderful animals – totally loving, trusting and affectionate. They are easy dogs who are bone-idle (no pun intended), intrigued by all the new adventures around them and really friendly to children and adults alike. They are often overlooked due to many preconceptions. Contrary to popular belief, they only need two twenty-minute walks per day and are very lazy. They would keel over if expected to go for a long run and would rather have a quick sprint and come back in to a nice comfy bed. They are often pictured chasing after things, but although you may have to watch them initially around smaller dogs, many live with little dogs, cats or even rabbits! They are very gentle with children – a characteristic which cannot be over emphasised. Sometimes families might go to the kennels with one child slightly overwhelmed and wary of the dogs. By the end of the morning, the calmness and affectionate nature of the dogs meant the child was out playing with the dog and did not want to go home.

It took me about a year with a little help from other people who had adopted a greyhound. One memorable event led to mum having a conversation with a lovely couple who had had their dog for several years. "We hardly know we've got her, she's no trouble" was the comment that would be quoted at mum endlessly. She must relent at some point, if only for a quiet life! It didn't take long before a sob-story led to us taking one of these needy souls more fully into our lives and into our home.

I was now working for an animal welfare charity in an office in London. Other staff brought their dogs into the office and the option of having a companion at work was something that played round and round in my head. It was agreed that because I could take a dog to work, if a 'cat-friendly' and 'train-friendly' greyhound came in looking for a home, then 'maybe' we could adopt him/her. It was a breakthrough I didn't ever expect. However, I'm sure these criteria were selected on the basis that such a greyhound would not materialise!

We tried a little girl called 'Bo' originally. We took her home to test her with the cats and she certainly did not pass the test! She reared up on her back legs and barked at our Manx cat, Freddie. Freddie had been selected to meet Bo based on the fact that he had previously lived with a dog. He was a ginger cat who had been found eating bread in our garden. He had fled when he first caught sight of us watching him, but gradually he came to trust us and it became quickly apparent that he was absolutely emaciated. He was so hungry but was wearing a collar. When we rang the owner, thinking that maybe he had been lost, the owner turned out to live a few doors down in a house backing onto our back garden. He told us that if we took him in, that he has kidney problems so had a tendency to wee and mess everywhere. That was appealing. We had no intention of taking him in. We already had four cats and if Freddie had a home, he should be looked after there! We delivered Freddie back to the house, walking round the block with him in a cat basket. He was taken inside. We walked back round, thinking it was done and dusted. As we opened the back door, a ginger Manx cat wandered in. We took him back several times only to find on one occasion when it was particularly cold and wet, that the family had moved away! I will never understand how anyone can live with themselves and simply abandon an animal. So we had five cats, but not, at this stage a 'cat-friendly', 'train-friendly' greyhound. I began to doubt whether I was asking too much.

And yet, not long after testing Bo, along came Storm. Storm had been picked up after being found wandering, scared and hungry. He had been due to be put to sleep. Councils give dogs seven days in the pound to see if they are claimed. If they are not claimed, they can be put down or rehomed. It really underlines the importance of micro-chipping your dog. With a simple chip which lasts a lifetime, the dog can be scanned and returned to you within the hour. Boroughs also do not liaise so if your dog crosses the boundary and ends up in a pound of which you are not aware, you might find your lost dog put-down before you can find him/her. If you do lose your dog, it is always best to ring every local borough to ensure they all have your contact details should a dog matching the description be picked up by their warden. It was clear that Storm was not going to be claimed and had been deliberately dumped. The dog warden who had picked him up had rung the local racing-dog trainer to see if they had lost a dog. They had not, but were due to bring a dog into the rescue kennel for rehoming. Thankfully, they offered to bring Storm along too – so here he was now looking for a home. He was the start of our life with greyhounds at home.

Storm was the perfect dog. He was clean from the start (apart from one accident overnight as a result of eating half a packet of gravy bones!). He loved his food and a cuddle and was asleep for most of the day. He did have to overcome a fear of men, footballs and pushchairs – no doubt as a consequence of his previous harsh treatment. He is also food orientated due to his history, but we worked around these things. Once he knows and trusts people, he is so gentle and loving. We know from looking up his records online that he raced twice in Ireland, before a year later being found wandering in England. His siblings had also been discarded (one sister found wandering in Yorkshire) and another ending up in Spain. I didn't want to think about what had happened to her. Greyhounds in Spain are notoriously badly treated and killed in barbaric ways. Rescue groups are becoming more and more active in rescuing the Spanish Galgo, the Spanish Greyhound used for hunting and abandoned and killed in their thousands at the end of their hunting season. Many Spanish people are appalled at this horrific treatment of their animals and do their best to save as many as they can. Like all animal welfarists, they are facing a huge mountain.

I took Storm to work with me, but only a few times! His nervousness meant he was not happy travelling on tubes or trains and he did cause one heart-stopping incident when someone on a stand waved a free newspaper at us and caused him to freak out, spin on the lead and have me over (in the middle of a road). Thankfully, we made it to the office, and with a park nearby, a quieter lunchtime walk calmed him down. He always remembered the route back to the office door though! This anxious event led to the conclusion that it was better for him to stay at home with mum, but that if she went out for the day, I would take him with me. On these occasions, I woke up at the crack of dawn and we drove to a station that both started and finished at the end of the line. This made life easier as I could walk through the city before the crowds descended. Coming home, of course, entailed a busier walk, but if I left slightly earlier (having arrived before most civilised people are even stirring), I was able to miss rush-hour. There is always the exception that proves the rule, however, and one night we had to squeeze onto a packed train due to a fault on the line. Mercifully, the train was running when we reached the station and we made it to a seat where I could tuck him under my feet. We did get some strange looks but he was a commuter just the same as everyone else (well, a greyhound version!).

Storm even became a star when I organised a campaign for greyhounds, presenting a letter to Downing Street accompanied by 'One Foot in the Grave' actress, Annette Crosbie, and author, Jilly Cooper, together with their own greyhounds! Storm tells all his friends how proud he was to have walked in St James' Park, travelled in a black cab passed the Palace of Westminster and walked down Whitehall! He was doing his bit for his greyhound friends and it was two paws up to those who had hurt him in the past! He was a good boy when Jilly Cooper took him on the lead, but my heart was in my mouth as there were quite a few squirrels about in the park! That would have been a headline we would not have wanted that day: 'greyhound drags author into lake, chasing squirrel'!

Many volunteers at the kennels had two greyhounds. It is noticeable how much they enjoy the company of their own kind and although

Storm visited each week, it had started to cross my mind that he needed a friend. Another dog might help him with his nerves. I had also been made redundant so was in the process of looking for another job (so it was only reasonable to point out that I had time to introduce another dog). I had a long battle on my hands again with an adamant mother.

Our second greyhound was Fleck. She was the most gentle and affectionate girl in the world. She had had four homes and distressingly been returned to kennels four times through absolutely no fault of her own. It is better that they come back to the rescue rather than be dumped elsewhere and this is emphasised most rigorously. However, her unlucky run seemed so unfair on her and it must cause the dogs such heart-ache and confusion. What must they think? Their racing days over and having found a warm and comfortable home with love and walks and adapted to a new life and family, they are only to be back in an enclosed kennel without the personal love of the one to whom they have given their loyalty. They deserve so much better.

Fleck was not readjusting well to kennel life. She wasn't eating, weight was dropping off her and knowing her now, she must have been desperate for her comfortable bed where she could lie with her legs in the air; and her walks where she could run free off the lead. We always instil in new adopters that keeping greyhounds on the lead is essential. They get enough exercise on the lead and it is better to keep them safe and stop them running off. But some dogs learn eventually and Fleck had clearly been taught in her previous homes. She even dragged you into the curb if she needed to go to the toilet – unheard of!

It turned out that she had also accidentally had a litter of puppies in her first home. I was utterly shocked and especially so when one of her puppies arrived at the kennels having been in many homes and different places herself. It really underlines the importance of generally having dogs neutered. Of course, there are a rare few valid exceptions, but in general, there are enough unwanted dogs waiting for homes in this country alone as it is, without adding to this number. It is pleasing when rescues do this simple operation as a matter of course, particularly with so many greyhounds needing homes. Fleck's baby, Lady, was a wonderfully playful and amusing character with traits we saw reflected in her mother. After unsuccessfully trying to persuade my mum to reunite Fleck with her daughter; Lady found a wonderful home and we were told she also goes into the curb to 'do her business' – amazing! It is fortunate that the beautiful little Lady fell on her feet in the end – she certainly was one of the lucky ones.

Fleck was such a friendly and placid girl, but she did have an affinity with muddy water. Frequently she would rise from the depths like a hippo in disguise, stinking mud and pond water dripping from every part of her body, a huge smile on her face. The more we shouted 'no', the more she looked over her shoulder while slowly sinking into the mud, grinning widely as the stinking water came over her, leaving just her head exposed! She would then splash around, before leaping up and doing a few circuits, showing off her speed in front of the other breeds, all of whom she met with wagging tail and gentle enthusiasm. Her zest for life, however, led to the revelation that she had a tendency to be a tad accident prone.

And so we came to Will. It all started while we were at the vet with Fleck following her latest escapade playing in the forest and splitting her dew claw, the thumb-like claw that sits near the wrist on the front legs. Greyhounds are notorious wimps and she was screaming so much when the vet tried to clip off the offending segment that it was decided a mild sedation would be required. Fleck was splayed out on the floor of the waiting room and the procedure was quick and painless. While we waited for her to wake up again, the phone rang.

Chapter Two:

"I know just the people"

"Is she dead"?

"No. She is asleep – she has had a claw removed, although she generally doesn't need sedating to have an excuse to find her bed"!

"Really? Greyhounds need so much exercise don't they?"

If we had a pound for everyone who thought that greyhounds need marathon walks, we would be richer than Simon Cowell (a huge dog-lover I understand!). As has already been said, Greyhounds only need two twenty minute walks per day and sleep for the rest of the day. It is necessary to repeat this all the time because it might encourage people to adopt these dogs. Dispelling the myths is essential in the battle to finding these beleaguered creatures the homes they deserve.

Meanwhile... Lisa the veterinary nurse was on the telephone.

"So you have found a greyhound wandering?"

Our ears pricked up with a mixture of dread, trepidation, concern and the realisation that we could perhaps help, or more accurately, become involved. Little did we know that the unfolding conversation before us would ultimately lead to a triple canine adventure with an emotional rollercoaster of an uphill ride along the way.

"So he's a male greyhound with brown and black markings, a dirty collar and he was running across the roads"?

Mum and I exchanged worried glances. Not having experienced much life beyond kennels, Greyhounds very rarely have any road sense and if he was running loose, he had the potential to cause a serious accident, causing damage to himself and anyone who was on the road at the time.

"He crossed the road by following some people on the crossing? What... he waited for the lights to turn red and the people to cross when the green man was flashing?" went the one-sided conversation from the veterinary nurse.

He sounded like a very intelligent dog!

"I know just the people who can help you – they are sitting here with a greyhound and volunteer for a greyhound rescue centre".

I wondered what we were going to encounter. At the time, I just assumed he would be microchipped and returned to his owners, who would surely be frantically looking for him and overjoyed to be reunited with their lost hound.

By this stage, Fleck was up and walking towards the door! She was making her great escape while she could and was not hanging about to listen to the conversation! The veterinary practice was due to close so the lady and her son who had picked up the wandering greyhound could not bring him to that particular practice to scan him for a microchip. The microchip would reveal his owner.

We arranged to meet at the animal hospital which is open 24 hours per day. We returned Fleck home for a further sleep and headed off to the hospital. Reality was starting to strike home. What on earth were we going to do if he was not chipped? However, we were now involved and would do our best for this dog. Knowing how many thousands of greyhounds need homes in the UK, we would do everything in our power to ensure he did not go into a pound. Certain breeds stand more of a chance than others in pounds and rescue centres; and at this time, the odds were not in a greyhounds' favour. I was not going to be responsible for sending a dog to a pound to face an uncertain future nor risk him disappearing into the system, only to be put to sleep at a later date. We had to be his voice. Of course, this is easier said than done!

Anyway, hopefully he would be chipped and his joyful owners would happily be reunited with their pampered pet before the hour was through.

We arrived early and after a few anxious minutes when we thought the dog might have escaped on the journey or done a runner whilst getting into the car, a black four-by-four car pulled into the car park. It contained a little boy called 'Will', his mum and a brindle greyhound. Will explained that he was calling him 'Sunny'. Will had spotted Sunny running around on the main road near his house and had then seen him heading down the hill to the next main shopping area. He verified what we had heard on the phone – that people were crossing the road at the lights and he had waited and followed them.

It was clear that Will had a soft-spot for Sunny. He was cuddling him and the dog was striking up a bond with him.

I immediately looked in Sunny's ears for any sign of tattoos which would have been another method to enable us to search for his identity and owner. Alternatively, it would have allowed us to trace the kennels through which he had been adopted. However, he had no earmarks. All racing greyhounds which are officially registered to race have tattoos in their ears. The general rule of thumb is that if both ears are tattooed, the dog has been born in Ireland, whereas if one ear is tattooed, the dog is English bred. A change in racing rules now means that dogs must be microchipped, but at this time the tattoo was the main method of identification. However, with nothing in his ears, we were left unsure of his age and without any idea about where he may have come from. It did, however, tell us that he was not a registered ex-racing (or even currently racing) greyhound.

Will was holding Sunny and we filed into reception where we were taken around to the side waiting area while the vet went to get the scanner. Will's mum said they would have kept him themselves if they had not had two dogs already. They had put Sunny in the garden while they tried to find out what to do next.

After another nail biting wait, the scanner was produced and ran over Sunny from head to tail. There was no microchip. We tried again in case we had missed it but the 'bleep' we all hoped to hear did not materialise. He was wearing a red collar which had paint stains spattered over it – and there was no tag attached. In hindsight, we should have twigged that this meant he was not the much loved pet we had hoped, but at the time we just wanted him to find his owner.

The vet said they would take him into the hospital where the van would come and collect him and take him to a kennels. I had visions of a Cruella Deville type character who would turn up and remove the unwanted dogs from the premises. We glanced up and saw that Will was silently crying in the corner. Perhaps he had had the same thought or just knew that Sunny would be worried and frightened being bundled into another van with more people with whom he was not familiar. I had to ask the question. Would he be given seven days and then be put to sleep? The answer was expected: if the dogs can be rehomed they have a chance after seven days, but with the numbers of greyhounds and Staffies looking for homes, the likelihood of this opportunity would diminish.

It is so tragic – each individual is irreplaceable and deserves a chance to enjoy this world, but human stupidity and sheer irresponsibility means stray animals are simply running on their luck. Not only are they left to wander, scared and frightened in a dangerous world where traffic hazards and unsavoury characters might render them in peril; but even when they are taken into a so-called 'safe' environment, they are still running the gauntlet.

We could not do it. We could not risk him being put to sleep before his time. He was a lovely boy and his life was precious to him. The only problem was that our local greyhound stadium had closed and with the number of surplus greyhounds awaiting homes, there was no space at the kennels for him.

Nevertheless, it was decided that we would put him in our car and do our best for him. He had clearly grown even more attached to Will, even during the short time that he had looked after him, and would not leave his side. I had brought a lead with me so he was securely fastened to us (he wasn't going to be allowed to run off again!), and we went back outside. We waved goodbye to Will and his mum and then

14

opened our car boot. We then encountered a problem as he would not jump in the car. He dug his heels in, did not want to go and started reversing away from the car. He was very strong on the lead, unusual for a greyhound, but was stubbornly and adamantly refusing to move himself towards the boot of the car. We couldn't blame him could we – he had only just met us, did not know where he would be going next and was being put into a strange car. After much negotiation and tugging, I decided that I would have to lift him. Greyhounds are so placid that I did not even contemplate that this would be an issue. I have lifted many greyhounds, all of whom let you do it without a struggle or a backwards glance. This would be the only way of getting him into the car. However, this boy was having none of it. There is always the exception that proves the rule and after expecting a subservient, resigned attitude, I was rather taken aback when he growled and lashed out. Somehow I maintained my grip on his lead, but the option of hoisting him into the car was quickly discarded! I had not bothered to bring a muzzle with me because Greyhounds are just not like this! After a lot more pulling and pushing and a heated debate between Sunny and myself, we eventually agreed that the best course of action was for him to get into the car. Perhaps this boy needed to make decisions for himself.

We made the brief car journey home thinking we would keep him with us at home temporarily while we made the calls to report a found 'lost' dog. Mum was not keen on having another dog in the house and although I was quite keen to have him there, I was worried about pushing mum too far. I rang every council in the area, every vet practice and every police station. I called the other greyhound rescue centres in the area. During every call, I received the same answer: "nothing has been reported". Now what were we going to do? He would have to stay with us overnight while we continued to think of options. Some councils took my details, others were only interested in moving me on and telling me that they had not had reports of such a dog missing on their systems. Nobody actually wanted to offer this poor dog a sanctuary or any help.

We let him sleep in the hall on that first night and determined to face the hurdle of what to do with him the next morning. He was totally clean overnight so it was clear that he must have been used to living indoors. The only disturbance was a sudden loud noise in the night when we heard thundering footsteps on the stairs. My mum and I charged out of our respective bedrooms to be greeted by a wagging tail and a little expectant face. He ended up settling down to sleep outside our bedroom doors and happily curled up on the landing all night. Despite the car altercations, he was such a loveable dog who had been through a rough experience and needed understanding and love (as well as a good dinner). He wasn't emaciated but he was certainly thin and needed to put on a considerable amount of weight.

We were still calling him Sunny. However, something about the name did not seem to suit him. He had not had a sunny time and we liked the old fashioned names for dogs! There had been some brilliant names at the kennels recently. Most memorably, the names that stuck out for us were Rodney and Trevor! Some people disagree, but who on earth would want to be called "Rover"?! We tried out several options and then it occurred to us that we were not the only people who had been involved in this rescue mission. Another human had been fundamental. We would call him 'Will' after the little boy who had initially found him.

We introduced Will to our two greyhounds. Mum went off to the forest with him so that we were off territory. Will was quite strong on the lead and did not seem to know how to behave. Perhaps he had never been walked before. If only he could talk and let us know his history. Anyway, we had absolutely no worries about the introductions. It would be a breeze. Fleck was as placid and gentle as a lamb and loved everyone and everything she met. Once she had gone charging after a Jack Russell puppy, leaving us standing with our hearts in our mouths. They disappeared over a ditch with us yelling in the distance. The next moment, Fleck reappeared, jumped the ditch and ran back towards us with the puppy in hot pursuit! Fleck would love Will and would welcome him, tail wagging. Storm would be fine too. We walked regularly with other greyhounds and he loved their company. I took Storm and Fleck and we met in the forest clearing. True to form, Fleck ran over, sniffed him and her tail rose in the air. It wagged frantically with the excitement of meeting a new friend. Storm was the next to meet him. He sniffed him and then ran over to cock his leg up a tree. He and Will sniffed the same smells and the same pieces of grass. They were nose to nose with absolutely no problems. This was going to be a doddle. We took them for a long walk and then walked into the house with them as we had been advised.

Then the problems started. Storm growled and lashed out. He did not want him there. We took them in the garden to see if that would help ease the situation. Fleck was so excited, running around and Will seemed to relish seeing a dog of his own kind. Perhaps this was the first time he had ever encountered another greyhound. Had he even seen any other dogs before? Fleck was absolutely wonderful and they sniffed around the garden together. Storm, however, was not having any of it. Now, this added an extra dilemma. We thought we would give it some time. Perhaps Storm would snap out of it, accept him and bond with him in the end. Then maybe mum would relent and we could keep him! That would solve everything as no one else seemed to want him! Not a single council had contacted us and so he was obviously not going to be claimed. Will was clean again overnight and slept outside our bedroom doors once again. We tried again the next day. Two more days with Storm wearing a muzzle and being totally unhappy followed. Will did not retaliate when Storm bared his teeth at him which was just as well as Storm was letting him know in no uncertain terms that Will was not welcome. We had never seen Storm so depressed and unsettled, but poor little Will was very careful around him, which was good considering the nightmare he had been whilst we had tried to get him into the car. Absolutely no progress was being made. Storm was indifferent or even accepting of Will whilst out on walks, but in the house, he would not even let Will walk past him. We could not blame him. He had found his security with us and his past was still haunting him. He must have felt his new found life was under threat.

What could we do but try and find somewhere for him? There was no room at the kennels, but there was a kennel that was in the same lane as the kennels with which we were linked. It was being used as a holding kennel, keeping the dogs from the stadium that had been surplus to requirements after its closure until there was a space for them to move into the rehoming kennels. Space was at a premium but there was a gap. The kennel owner was contacted by our kennel owner and he agreed to take him until we could either trace the owner or think what to do. I still had not had any response from the many phone calls to councils, veterinary practices or any of the other places I had thought might have known his identity.

We took him to the holding kennels and thought we would keep him there until the seven days were up. None of the councils had explained the process of what to do if you find a lost dog. I now know that councils, at that time, have to hold the dog for seven days if it is in one of their kennels, but if the finder of the dog wishes to keep the dog in their care, they have to be issued with a legal notice which lasts for 28 days. Therefore, the best way to adopt a stray is to have it kennelled by the local council and if it is not claimed after seven days, it can then be legally adopted. However, at the time we believed the seven days applied to us reporting him as found. We had not been told differently when we rang the councils so were just going to hold him until the required time period had elapsed. We could then decide what to do.

Whenever we drove past the holding kennel, we thought of Will inside. Storm was relieved to have him depart, but although we were more relaxed without the potential of World War Three in our house, we worried about Will and how he must be feeling. The poor dog had been presumably kicked out of his home, been wandering, found young Will, been given to us, and now we had let him down again by handing him on yet again. We had reports that he could not get onto the kennel beds and so was being lifted. He had clearly not been in kennels before and had not raced so did not know the routine of such a place. It was a kennel where the dogs were let into grass paddocks, but not walked. Would he know what was expected of him or even what to do? Would he be frantically looking for an escape route? Perhaps he was just happy to have a place of his own where he was fed and exercised. We tried to block out our anxieties while we waited for the time to lapse. What were we going to do?

We were spurred into making a decision by a phone call saying one of the kennel hands had been bitten by Will as he was lifting him onto the bed. This is unheard of in greyhounds – they are so affectionate and gentle. It is one in a million that is ever a worry around human beings. We know of greyhounds living with babies, toddlers and children of all ages. Why did we have to encounter a wild unruly beast in a greyhound costume? They said they would not trust him around other dogs or other humans and we needed to go and collect him. We knew he had been fine with Fleck and it had not been Will who was the problem in our house.

It then occurred to me that perhaps Storm would be ok with Will if he was neutered. Will had not been 'done' and this may have been a factor as Storm was defending his territory. Storm was very good with most dogs when out on his walks, but if he took a dislike to another dog, the common denominator seemed to be that the dog was an unneutered male. So this was the next plan of action. The holding kennel agreed to keep him until the day of the neutering operation. The seven days were up so we would have to find him a permanent rescue place, keep him ourselves or find him another home.

As we entered the gate of the holding kennel, we had a sense of foreboding. How would he react to us now? Would he be a savage and uncontrollable furry nightmare who would pin us to the floor and tear us limb from limb? He had been moved up to a block at the far end of the site and we waited, chewing what was left of our nails, for him to be brought out to us. He walked out, pulling a bit, legs splayed apart and neck bowed as he tried to break free and weaving from left to right on the lead. Then he caught sight of us. He gave a little yelp and, tail spinning from side to side, he rushed towards us. This was the moment of truth. He leapt up at me, front paws on my shoulders and leant into me, so pleased to see us. The kennel owner looked on in astonishment: "he likes you" was all he could say!

What a relief that Will was still the dog we had known. He had been so placid with us at home, apart from the car incident, but was a very fast learner and had quickly grasped the idea of getting in and out of the car without problems. However, the bond he was forming with us was not going to make it any easier. We still had the friction between Storm to contend with and did not think the minor break would have made any difference. However, we did not have to deal with that immediately as the operation was in store for Will that day. The vet was based half an hour away and the kennels used it for all neutering. They knew us well in there and we left Will in their care. It was a bit traumatic to leave him as he must have thought we were abandoning him again. He must have wondered what on earth was going on now while he was stuck in a small cage awaiting his surgery in the vet back-room.

Neutering is such a quick and easy operation, especially for the boys. If only governments would implement it for stray populations, we would not have so many unwanted, abandoned, suffering and homeless animals. In the long term, it would save money too as kennelling fees for strays and the potential hazards that stray animals encounter around the world can be very financially costly. It is a sad necessity that this is the answer. Of course I would love to have the offspring of my dogs forever, but for greyhounds and other surplus dogs, this would be ridiculous for the millions of homeless animals who I would be depriving of a home. There are more dogs than homes already and human lack of care has exacerbated this into a crisis. Dogs are abused, neglected and cast out all over the world and endure unimaginable hardships out on the streets. Neutering would stop the cycle in its tracks and start to alleviate the strain on rescue organisations globally.

So we were doing the right thing, without any conceivable doubt. We went to collect him at about 5.30pm and despite all our anxieties, he had been fine. We brought him home and allowed him the evening and night to recover. He did mark a bit that night as we found in the morning when we came downstairs to several stained radiators, but we felt the anaesthetic could have been a contributing factor. Mum was, of course, less understanding, but luckily we had a decorator in at the time so doors and walls had been stripped down ready to be painted. Once the stains had been blitzed by disinfectant and a coat of paint, no one would be any the wiser. I reminded mum that Will had been spotlessly clean when we had him at home before.

We knew we had to try Storm again. We repeated the 'off-territory' introductions. Once again, they were fine together in the forest; but in the house, Storm continued the growling.

Will was eating well, although he wasn't used to dog biscuits or tripe. He would quite readily sit in anticipation of a human biscuit, but dog biscuits were a complete mystery to him. He would sit and give paw of his own volition, raising first the left paw and then the right over and over again. He was desperate to please us and we took this as a sign that someone had loved him once. However, it was a strange type of 'giving paw'; almost an obsession. Will was clearly loving his walks. He wasn't used to the lead so we wondered again whether he had ever been walked at all in the past. It certainly did not seem like it. Everything was new to him. Other dogs were a novelty or a bit frightening to him. Trees, ponds, grass and flowers were fascinating with new smells and sights and worlds to explore. He would stand and gaze at things with incredulous enchantment. We kept the muzzle on him during these walks as we were not sure how he would react to other dogs. Sometimes he seemed to want to run over and play; other times he would retract and be quite bewildered by whatever was in front of him. We gave him a green orthopaedic bed and he slept in the kitchen during the day and in the hall at night.

It was turning into a situation where we were separating Storm and Will. Fleck, a little darling as always, could go quite happily between the two. Will was also absolutely fine with the cats, muzzle employed again initially. We had to keep Storm and Will apart; we also had to keep our cat Winnie apart from our other cat Molly! It was almost farcical!

We tried introductions and care again for a further week, but Storm was so unhappy having to wear his muzzle and continued to growl if ever Will came too close.

I phoned various contacts for help, targeting those who had had two males before. All had not had such a situation occur to them. It was so frustrating as it was solely Storm; and Will would not engage in any defence or respond at all! I then phoned a rescue organisation who have seventeen greyhounds living in their home. How do they manage!? She said they were mostly males and all got along fine. She had, however, had one incident where the dog had been unable to integrate.

We continued for a few more days before I finally decided to call the councils in one last attempt to relocate the previous owners. Surely he must have been loved; giving his paw and being so loveable, he must be the apple of someone's eye. He would whizz up and down the stairs, whereas some greyhounds, only used to kennel life and never having seen things that we take so much for granted, struggle on stairs at first. The fact that he would only eat tinned dog food, showed he had lived in a home and all this backed up the experience of the holding kennel. He was wearing the collar when found so maybe he belonged to a decorator who took him to work with him? He was thin, but perhaps he had been loose and running for a while which meant the weight had dropped off him.

Funnily enough, we had a decorator doing up our hall and my bedroom at the time. On one occasion, we left him in my bedroom, stripped of most of its furniture, while we went out with friends to a pre-arranged theatre show featuring a radio presenter we all enjoyed. We had debated about how we would be able to go but we figured Will would be unable to do much harm in an empty room. He would have to be ok while we had a little break. The worry of the unknown outcome and anxiety over what would happen, meant we enjoyed the outing and had a release from having to think about what to do for the best, at least for a few hours. Despite our feelings of guilt about leaving the dogs, we stayed on for fish and chips. When we got home, Will had dug up the carpet, but he had been clean. He was overjoyed to see us and hurled himself on us, leaping up and smothering us with cuddles, wrapping his front paws around us whilst standing upright on his back legs. Storm and Fleck were all tail wagging and excitement too; and were also spotless. They were always so good and laid back.

But the growling over Will was continuing. I was trying to switch off from the situation. Storm was distressed and this was upsetting in itself. Mum, who had not wanted even one dog (and who now had three!) had, however, been heard to say, " I love this little Will". She seems to have a lapse of memory over this comment, but I distinctly remember her saying it on many occasions when he was giving his paw or being generally endearing! However, it was impossible to keep the two dogs separated. If we were watching television, Will would be stuck behind the baby-gate and be very upset to be away from us. If he came in the room, Storm would go for him. If Storm was separated, he would also cry and become very distressed. So I made further calls to the councils, one of which I regretted and have blamed myself for afterwards (and ever since).

Chapter Three:

"I am going to prosecute you"

Our borough council had kept our details and not had any reports of missing brindle greyhounds. The next two were the same. Initially I could not get through to the fourth council, but on my second attempt, they said they would pass on my follow-up call to the dog warden who was on leave that day, but back tomorrow.

The following day, I was up at the kennels all day as I was every Friday. Will, Storm and Fleck stayed at home, but had been up there when we went up on other days. Will would go in an empty kennel until it was time to go home. I recall the end kennel, number twenty-six, being the kennel in which he spent a few hours waiting for us to finish looking after the other dogs, before going home again. He would stand gazing out of the bars, not sure what to do with himself and not attempting to sit on the bed. When in the kennel and a confined space, he could be slightly defensive, letting out a small rumbling growl with some people who he did not know and we therefore just warned people to be gentle with him. Otherwise he would give his paw and be happy to go for a walk around the field.

On one occasion, he had gone up there in mum's car, with me following on with another dog and his lady owner. I looked at Will in the boot in front of me and was so proud of him. He had been such a good boy, was so affectionate and although he had things to overcome, while we were at the kennels, we could forget the problems of introducing him to Storm. The lady's dog, Dara, had been adopted from the kennels and his owner wanted to visit in order to help out one morning. She did not drive and, as we had performed the homecheck, we said we would take them there. In the end, some months later, she ended up returning Dara through no fault of his own. Thankfully, he now has a wonderful home, but seeing dogs brought back to the kennels is always distressing. Of course, it is better that they come back than get passed on or pushed out, but we always wish the dogs to be settled once and for all when they find a home. At the time, his owner had commented that she would love to find an unclaimed dog and feel you could help it by offering a home. Little did she know! Part of me agreed – I would take in any animal and it had been so hard to convince mum to let me have a dog, that to have one land on your doorstep with no option but to take it in, was unbelievable; and yet, it was not easy. There was concern that the owner could come forward at any time and this meant uncertainty about making plans. In addition, he needed to adapt, work through his anxieties, stop pulling on the lead, stop whining and needed to socialise with Storm (as well as Fleck).

We had worked through Storm's anxieties and it is always so rewarding to see the progress that the nervous dogs, in particular, make once they settle and trust again. They have been through so much and yet they still love and trust once they get to know you. Their history will never leave them and makes them part of who they are, but the fact that they overcome their mistreatment and start to enjoy life and care again, repaying it in bucket loads, is an amazing credit to their characters. We could get there with Will, who was not nervous at all, but just needed to learn what was expected of him; if only Storm would accept him.

I had a sense of something hanging over me that Friday. Mum rang to say Will had been for a walk for over an hour. She had taken Storm and Fleck first and then Will on his own. I was a bit concerned as he had not long been neutered, but at least the walking would get some of the energy out of him.

My mobile rang at about 11am. "This is the dog warden...I was on leave yesterday".

"Yes, hello", I replied, "I just wanted to ring you again to check if the dog we have taken in has not been claimed?"

"You have found a dog"?

"I rang three weeks ago to report him found and nobody has claimed him. He is not getting on with one of my other dogs so, I know it's a long shot, but I just want to be sure he hasn't got a home".

If he had been my dog, I would have wanted the finder to call. I was sure this was all a waste of time anyway as the councils had my name and number and nobody had phoned. The next response was totally staggering.

"I am going to prosecute you – you did not report this dog as found and I have an owner for this dog", he retorted with the compassion, charm and helpfulness of an axe-murderer seeking out his next victim.

I was both shocked, filled with dread, and yet with a little bit of relief at the same time. Will could now be returned to his owner. Storm would be happy again and all would be well. I just hoped the owners were as excited as I would be if my precious canine friend was being returned to me. But what had he said? He said he was going to prosecute us?

We had done nothing but our best for the dog from the minute we became involved by a chance phone call to our vet as we sat with Fleck in the waiting room. We had taken in the dog, had him neutered and looked after him. We had reported him as 'found' to every local borough council in the area and prevented him being dumped on a rescue centre, already overrun with dogs. How could he be threatening prosecution?

I queried why I had not been contacted before and he said I had not reported it. By this stage, I was getting angry with him. This man was not doing his job properly and trying to cast the blame onto me. I told him that I had indeed reported it and that surely it was up to his staff to take my details and liaise together. This was not my fault and I was not going to accept any blame. Eventually he backed down and said he would ring the owner, explain the situation and why we had had Will neutered. After a nail-biting wait, he rang back subsequently to say the owners were not concerned regarding the neutering and he would meet me at the address now.

I was not happy with the demanding nature of his attitude. Instead of being grateful and clear on what was happening, he was accusative and aggressive. I was at the kennels until 3pm and had nothing but Will's interests at heart since we took him on board. Why could he not see that? He gave me the address and we agreed to meet there at 4.30pm.

Mum did a dummy run and reported back that the house was very dilapidated, had boarded up windows and was very run-down. I was starting to feel sick and full of concern, but then if the dog is loved, it doesn't matter what the house looks like. Perhaps it was newly bought which would explain the paint on his collar and the reason he was running loose, unsure as to where to go back. It was a huge concern though. What if they did not love him? But then why would they have reported him missing otherwise?

It was a strange day. I felt highs and lows and mixed emotions throughout the day. Perhaps we could visit him every now and again in his new home. I would take some food with me as a little gift for him and to welcome him back to his old home.

I arrived home and with a sense of oncoming dread, we watched the clock count down to 4pm when we had to leave and get in the car. Mum sat in the back with him laying stretched out across her lap. He continued to give his paw as he lay there and had his head in her arms. I was numb and robotic, going through the motions of doing what was necessary whilst feeling like this was not really happening. I drove, looking ahead. It was too heartbreaking to look at them in the back. We just had to return him and I had to start to detach. It was easier said than done and the drive seemed to go both quickly and yet in slow motion. As we pulled into his road, which was a main road, I was taking short breaths and just praying that we would see a happy reunion with a loving and devoted owner. As we continued down his street, we made encouraging noises to him to see if he showed a happy reaction. His lack of any noticeable awareness about where he was did not help to clarify how he would behave once he caught sight of his home and owner.

We pulled up a few doors along as we were early. Suddenly, the door of a house flew open and out ran a man. Behind him was a girl and they were drinking; loud music was playing. The windows were smashed with cardboard concealing the space and the paintwork and decor were filthy. Some old nets which had presumably once been white, hung at dodgy angles in the remaining windows. The door was old and wooden and did not seem to have a keyhole or doorbell. An old rusty padlock seemed to be the only way of securing it. Surely this could not be the house. I counted backwards along the street and to our utter horror, this seemed to tally with the number we had been given.

We contemplated going. But how could we do a runner? We had agreed to meet the warden who had our address; and perhaps the house was the wrong number; and perhaps the owner was desperate for their beloved and treasured boy.

Eventually the warden arrived. His hostility and arrogant manner was evident from the start. His sole concern was rules and regulations and there was no compassion for the dog. He took a photo of Will for his records and made no attempt to greet or pat him. He would not let us give the food, saying it was not good to change the diet as he would be fed what he was used to. The man was clearly forgetting that Will had been in our care (and that of the holding kennels) for the last three weeks and the diet would be being switched back to his original. He did notice that Will could do with more weight – and this, despite having filled out a bit with two regular meals per day whilst he had been with us. I took the opportunity to find out Will's original name; about the only piece of information the warden actually deemed to tell me.

"He's called, Matty". (I have changed this original name for my own purposes).

The warden knocked on the door and no one answered. I went to go, but the warden stood in front of me, threatening me again with prosecution if we did not return the dog. In hindsight, I do not know how we continued to stand there, but at the time, we were in a position where we did not have any choice. It was like a nightmare and the numbness in me continued as if an out-of-body experience was occurring. This must be happening to somebody else. After a couple more knocks on the door, with us holding our breath on the doorstep in the hope that it would not open, it was tentatively drawn back to reveal a twelve year old boy. He peered through the tiny gap and explained his mum was out and a funeral had taken place that day with the wake being held at the house. It all seemed very strange and, as we gazed into the house, I was filled with even more horror. There were bicycles up the stairs which had no carpet. The house looked ran-sacked and smashed. Not only were the stairs uncarpeted, but the floor of the hall was bare and the walls all chipped and unpainted. There were wooden floor boards on show in another room leading off the hall which I could just see through the door.

Meanwhile, the dog warden was reading the law to the twelve year old who was looking decidedly bored and uninterested. At no point did he look down to Will, who was standing with me, and show any sign of relief and joy at seeing his dog. Where was this boy's mother? Why wasn't she waiting for her dog, knowing we were coming? Anyone who loved their dog would be waiting on the road for the van to pull up and be ready to greet their beloved companion with treats and a big hug. But not this family. Our worst fears were starting to be realised...and I had made the call to put Will back into this situation.

The warden read the regulations like a robot and I took my chance to speak to the boy. He confirmed that the dog was a greyhound, aged three years and they had had him since he was six weeks old. I gave him some information with our phone number in case they needed our help as a rescue organisation in the future. By this stage, I could not care less what the dog warden said or did. I had found this dog and looked after him and I was going to do my best to make sure the boy knew how to care for him. I asked for his mobile number which the warden wrote down. The warden had refused to give me the name of the owner due to data protection. It was clear that whatever rules were necessary for him to adhere to, he was taking great delight in being as obstructive and difficult as he could. He had no idea about care for animals and was simply a computer in human form, carrying out his duties with an icy detachment that made the depths of the Arctic Ocean look like the Tropics of Central Africa. We had done our best and yet were being punished for our care.

The warden wrote the number down incorrectly and I had to ask him to change it. Why was he being so incredibly inconsiderate and nasty? There was no kindness or care in the man whatsoever. Will was pushed into the house and he was wearing a collar we had given him. I handed his red collar back to the boy who said, "I remember this". I had hoped we would be able to give him a goodbye cuddle, but even this was denied for him (and for us).

Considering Will had only been missing for less than three weeks, this was unbelievable. The collar was the only thing the boy remembered. What about the living, breathing, sentient and loving creature who they had not known was alive or dead for nearly a month? The warden asked what they fed Will and said they needed to feed more. Then he said he ought to be tagged and he would prosecute if the dog went missing again. This was obviously his favourite word and his ego clearly needed boosting, even if it was only he, himself who respected the power he was bestowing upon himself. His self-esteem must have been so low that he needed to exert control. But why did Will have to suffer as a result of this loser?

Thankfully, I have since heard that dog wardens are not all like this and his approach was not universal! We were incredibly unlucky to be forced into a situation with someone who clearly could not give a damn about animal welfare or the efforts of those who do. Many dog wardens around the country battle in incredibly difficult situations to save as many dogs as possible by working with rescues and doing their best, showing much more feeling and compassion. Of course, more needs to be done to save dogs that end up in pounds. Too many dogs are put down across the UK when they cannot be returned to their owners. Too many dogs are abandoned or end up with irresponsible human beings who do not have any regard for those who work tirelessly to protect animal welfare. Campaigners and animal rescuers try to step in to stop thousands of individual dogs being killed when they end up in pounds. Fortunately, the dog warden we crossed paths with no longer works in the field. We learnt later that others had had upsetting dealings with this man. His replacement has been praised by his manager for his work in trying to home strays that come into his care.

As we came down the path, I felt totally sick and in a daze. Suddenly, we were surrounded by neighbours, who seemed to appear from every door and who independently gave us the same analysis of the situation.

"You are not seriously putting that dog in there are you?" said one neighbour.

The warden, with his predictable ruthlessness said "it is their property" – and then turning to us said: "I could prosecute you for having him neutered".

Not this again. And Will was not an "It"?... – Who was this so-called man?

I turned to the neighbour: "what do you mean?"

"You must be mad to put that dog back in there – they kick him, beat him and starve him", came the response.

I dissolved into tears. What had we done? My poor darling Will – with his little paws and his eagerness to please; his enjoyment of his walks and his pleasure in the food we gave him.

I turned to the warden in desperation: "you can't put him back in there".

"It is their property; I am going to prosecute you" he clinically retorted.

Mum lost her temper. "That's three prosecutions now, what else? Can't you listen to what they are telling you?"

"If that dog goes missing, you will be our first port of call" was his automatic reply.

I pointed out that we were not likely to go in and steal him, tempting as it was. The neighbours said he had been looked after for a while by the owners' mother, but she had taken him back. The owner was a destructive alcoholic who was not taking care of the family or dog.

Whilst we were talking, the twelve year old had come out of the house, smirking. Will was in there somewhere, but just left alone, despite being missing. Will was only three years old and must have known nothing but suffering. He needed someone to end the outrage that was his cruelty. Somebody had to care about him, make a difference for him and not allow him to go back to this life. Why was the warden so dismissive, patronising and cruel? He was now accusing me of only being upset because I wanted the dog. I made it clear that I am involved with a rescue kennel where I could have any greyhound I wanted. I am involved because I care about their welfare; and the welfare of the dog I am crying over is my only criterion for my misery. His response was as heartless as ever. He defensively said that he had a degree so he must therefore care about animals too. I personally could not see how the two statements were linked. I had a Masters Degree, but whether or not anyone has any university qualifications, this is a totally irrelevant factor for the grief over the welfare of my poor 'Will'.

The hope for a joyful reunion was now a distant memory. The neighbours said they had tried to get the dog out but the authorities had not acted. The warden dismissed this out of hand. How could he be so wicked? His attitude was summed up in his final statement which was: "what do you expect me to do about it on a Friday afternoon"?

Another neighbour was commenting that Will must have thought he was in heaven while he had been with us. I asked them if they would be willing to try and get him out. I gave out my number and they promised to try.

Mum and I were left reeling. I was so upset. I just wanted to be near Will. We drove home and rang the national charity responsible for acting in these situations. I was told to await their call. I just had to do something.

We drove back to the house and walked up and down. This journey back was the first of many drive-bys in which we desperately tried to see Will. The neighbour who had promised to try and get the owner to give Will up did not ring. Perhaps they were pacifying me or trying to be kind by giving hope. But this had been a false hope and only served to make me more and more unhappy.

We did hear from the welfare inspector who was aware of Will and his plight. She felt that it was a 'golden opportunity missed', a comment which left me in pieces. I was wracked with pain by the fact that he was suffering, that I could not get in to get him out, and that I had put him into the house. If only I had not made the call. If only...if only...

The inspector promised to go and check on him in a few weeks, allowing time for our care of him to diminish. It was a waiting game with no light at the end of the tunnel. If Will was to be removed, he would have to suffer more in the process. I said that a home would be available with me if she ever managed to remove Will. Knowing that so many dogs already need homes in this country, I felt this might be an incentive to do something. He would not be another homeless number, taking up a valuable kennel space, but would be adopted immediately. I would deal with fitting him back in (and with mum!) if it ever happened.

It was so frustrating. As we drove past, we hoped he wasn't suffering and that he wasn't hungry. We never saw him and the agony of the situation often had me devastated. I would think of his little feet; the cross-paths place in the forest where we had stood and chatted about him whilst he stood there on a lead as we told the owner of a spaniel all about him. The green bed was relegated to the garage as I could not bear to see it vacant when it was available for him. What was he sleeping on? Did he have any comforts? Now he knew what a comfortable bed, nice walk and tasty dinner consisted of, would he be suffering even more?

We decided to take a train journey as the track ran along the back of the house. We got a return ticket to give us the chance to look twice, on the outgoing and return journey. The train was quite fast and picked up speed quickly, but from what we could see, the garden was as unkempt and destroyed as the house with no sign of Will anywhere.

Someone also had the idea of ringing the owner. Would she want to get rid of him if we offered to buy him? We had the son's number from our conversation at the door, and he passed us to his mother. Mum exchanged pleasantries before making the offer, claiming our friend had never seen a dog like him and was really keen to offer him a home and would, of course, pay. Of course, the kennels were full of brindle dogs looking for homes, but she just said 'no'. Another hope blown out of the water. The inspector was our last lifeline.

Chapter Four:

"Can we get him out?"

Going back to the kennels was a weird and surreal experience. Kennel number twenty-six where he had peered out had a haunting, vacant stillness about it. It was hard to see any kennel empty as we knew there was a dog that was so near, and yet so far, who would benefit from being in it. Of course, any space in a greyhound rescue kennel is filled within days, but nevertheless, I could not help thinking about Will, who most certainly needed rescuing.

I took to driving past the house at any opportunity, driving myself mad in the process. It was lucky that the house was on a main road, meaning I wouldn't get strange, quizzical glances from curtain-twitchers every time I appeared! Most of the time, I would see nothing. The hoped for figure of a brindle greyhound charging out of the house and stopping the traffic in front of me did not materialise, funnily enough! There also seemed to be no movement in the house as the windows remained smashed and the door was always shut. It was unclear whether I would even know if the family had moved away and if Will was still there. I tried to vary the times that I went past. I was helping out at the kennels more often and could therefore go home via Will's road. When I was asked to cover the early morning shift, I went down his road at 7am. Again, the house was still. One time there was a padlock on the door. Perhaps the family were out? Or had they left the house? The next day, I went past at 4.30pm. Again, there was nothing to convey any existence in the house or any sign of a dog. The padlock was, however, no longer on the door.

Another time, I went by at 1pm. There was nothing to be seen. I had to be a bit careful as I could not be totally intent on looking into their house! It was a bus route as well as a busy main road so despite my attempts at gesturing buses on as I pulled up outside, the majority of the time, I could only manage looking at the house as I approached, and a quick glance to the left as I went by. On one occasion, I saw who I presume was the woman owner. She was chatting to a neighbour in the doorway, but there was no sign of Will. From what I could see, the house looked as derelict and broken as it had when we put Will back.

We waited for six weeks, then seven, but still heard nothing from the inspector. I rang again and gave the details she had given me so that they would put me through to her. I waited again for her to ring me back. It is so frustrating that so much time and waiting is involved. Surely in these situations, action is best taken swiftly to achieve the best results. I hate having things hanging over my head and have always preferred to do things as soon as I get them. I cannot see the point of hanging around, thinking about doing something when you can just get on and do it, and then forget about it. I was always regarded as a workaholic in school and in the office, but it is more to do with the fact that I do not want to spend time worrying about doing something, thus doubling the effort. By the time I have wasted the energy putting something off and gathering more things to do in the process, I figure that you may as well get it off your back as soon as you get it! So having to wait for a phone call was infuriating. Instead of gathering momentum to get this poor dog out, I was having to endure a pointless wait in which I would be thinking about what the inspector might say. It was necessary to reign in any incumbent thoughts which might intrude the brain and give rise to too much hope or too much despair. Sometimes I would think that she had got him out, but then I knew if she had done so, I would surely have received a phone call.

I had kept my mobile close by me ever since we had put Will back into the house. Just maybe it would ring one day with good news. Any news would have been a bonus at this point. The not-knowing was the most heartbreaking thing. If it was this agonising for Will, I cannot even imagine how people get through the day when their children go missing.

At times during the day, it would break into my consciousness and interrupt whatever I was doing. I felt Will was still in the house, but I did not know for sure. A frustrating thing about waiting for the inspector to call you back is that you have no idea when they will call or where you will be when they do. I had visions of being in the car and being unable to answer my phone, consequently missing the call. When eventually she did call, I was out at a rare reunion with former work colleagues. I had just had a conversation about how I was trying to get Will out when my phone rang. The pub was noisy and because the number is retained, I was not sure who it was. I had received several spam calls, only adding to my irritation over the past few weeks. If this was someone else trying to sell me double glazing, they were asking for the phone to be hurled into the nearest cess-pit!

When I heard the inspector's voice, time seemed to stand still. This was the call I had been waiting for and yet I could hardly hear her! I frequent pubs only occasionally when meeting up with old friends and, having yet to find a drink I enjoy, I don't drink and generally prefer to go out to experience places and sights if I have the option. I enjoy a good debate, but am not so keen on small-talk. This pub had supposed to be quiet, but unfortunately our crowd was being drowned out by a noisy leaving party for someone retiring from the local fire station!

"Hold on.." I said, "I am just in a pub and will go outside".

I happened to be trapped between people at the head of the table. I needed to get outside so I could hear the call and make sure I had covered all the concerns and questions I needed to ask. I decided that the best course of action was to push, push hard and make a dash for it! I was not going to linger any longer! I did not stop to look behind at any potential casualties I had left in my wake, performed a few movements worthy of the best contortionist to break free from the masses and made my break for the door. The party was in full swing behind me, but the pavement outside was peaceful and somewhat deserted. I went round the corner to ensure I was on my own and apologised for the commotion!

The welfare officer was kind and understood my pain and predicament, but her hands were tied from above. I could not believe this.

"So can we get him out"? I asked, tentatively, fearing the answer.

"The greyhound is still in the home. He looks thin and I would prefer that he did not stay there" came the response.

So he was still there. At least I knew that he was definitely alive and his location remained the same.

"I'm afraid I can't remove him without witness statements from the neighbours" she said.

"What about if I try to get witness statements from the neighbours?" I asked.

"I would need these in order to proceed – if they would like to contact me, I can go in again..."

"So you won't go in again without this?"

"No"

This was ridiculous. A dog, my poor little Will, was in need, it was best for him not to be in the home, he was thin, but nothing could be done?

I was shaking and so upset but I had to go back into the pub, act as if I was ok for the rest of the evening and save my tears for when I got home. I was not in the mood for having to cheer the retiring fire officer or talk about Eastenders. The evening passed in a bit of a daze and I was glad to be sitting down as my legs felt like they belonged to somebody else. Somehow I got through the rest of the time, made my excuses and made it home. My emotional front dissolved as soon as I walked over the threshold and I shed some tears while I relayed the conversation back to mum. It was utterly devastating and I still cannot understand why it is so hard to get a dog out of a home in which he was not being treated well. We were offering a home to him and yet we could not help him.

We had just started supporting a charity in which service men and women had become involved in rescuing dogs from Afghanistan. This amazing and awe-inspiring work had begun when a Royal Marine serving in an out-post of Afghanistan had befriended a stray dog. Dog fighting is a practice horrifically used as entertainment in Afghanistan, and the marine was not prepared to sit back and watch human beings abuse animals for fun. Dogs are caught and stored ready for the fighting, bound with wire and have their ears and tail cut off to prolong the fight. Bitches in season are often tied up and subjected to forced matings in order to provide more puppies for fighting. Street dogs have to survive in horrendous conditions. Not only do they have to endure the cold Afghan nights and scorching heat of the day; they have to avoid bombings and war, scavenge on the streets, and avoid the predatory humans so intent on using them for their sadistic entertainment. I can never understand what pleasure humans get in torturing and hurting animals. Despite the numerous and unending justifications, at the end of the day hunting, bullfighting, circus acts, shooting parties and any animal-inflicted-suffering for human gratification is simply undertaken because people enjoy the practice and do not see the individual suffering-being in front of them. It baffles me. Why there are not more laws against causing animal cruelty for 'fun,' I will never understand.

Anyway, the founder of the charity protecting the Afghan strays had ended up, unintentionally, looking after and safeguarding many dogs in the compound during his time in Afghanistan! Dogs had gravitated towards the sanctuary he provided and one particular dog, the dog he had initially set free from the fight, had attached himself especially to the marine. At the end of his service, the marine had been unable to walk away from his four-legged companions and vowed to bring them home. He could not abandon them to go back to their lives of hardship and suffering. Despite all the odds, remote location and hostile circumstances, he had achieved the unimaginable and some of the dogs were living the life of riley in the UK, USA and elsewhere. Stray dogs can often be a source of solace to those on active service and it became apparent that other people had found themselves in a similar situation. This triggered the formation of the charity, Nowzad Dogs, and the sterling work undertaken by this charity also includes the founding of a sanctuary and work to improve the welfare of animals in Afghanistan by working with the local people.

Why was it such a struggle for me to do this for a dog ten minutes away when it was possible to bring animal friends home from one of the most war-struck places on earth?

I decided that the next step would be to compile some letters to post to the neighbours. I knew the addresses from having returned Will and could miss out Will's number from the mailout. I wrote an anonymous letter stating that I was aware of a dog living in a house nearby who was being, at best neglected, and at worst, downright abused. I had set-up an email address and asked for them to email me any witness statements they might have. I gave them the alternative option of ringing the inspector in the hope that this would trigger her to go in again. I posted them near to Will's home and sat and waited. I checked the email address obsessively, but nothing came through. I guessed the neighbours who had told me about him would all be too worried to come forward for fear of having to give evidence or be held to account for their statements. I could understand this in a way as it would be a nightmare to suffer retribution from a hostile neighbour, but it did not help Will and it did not help me to protect him.

Another thing that did not help me was the apathy of those who professed to care for animals. We had taken up walking with one lady and her dog, but during one of our walks, very soon after we had had to put Will back into the home, we were talking about his case and received the dismissive response that "you can't save every dog". I have had this said to me on a few occasions and I am always surprised, angry and confused by such a statement. I appreciate that you cannot save every dog, but this doesn't mean you should not try! Moreover, I was not attempting to save every dog, I wanted to save the one individual dog who I was involved with and knew about. I could not walk away from him, knowing he was there. If I did not try to help him, no one else was going to do so. Every single animal is precious and we all need to do our bit to stop tragedy and step in if we see something that needs to change. It is obvious that one individual human cannot save every dog on planet earth, but this point is not worth making, especially in such a context. Every individual helped is a whole life that does not have to endure suffering. If someone felt that about you, I bet the attitude would not be: "well, you can't save every human". Imagine if someone knew you were suffering yet did absolutely nothing to help you; or even try to help you. We hope others will assist us if we are in dire straits and it is no different for individual animals who rely on others to help them. It's even more poignant if the one who knows you are suffering, yet does nothing, had some involvement in putting you into the circumstances which contributes to the suffering. I suspect that if our lady 'friend' fell down a huge crevice in the street, she would be outraged if people walked by overhead saying, "well, you can't help everyone"! In that moment, I was pretty tempted to set this up as an experiment!

I wasn't even asking for them to do anything. I simply needed an empathetic ear and acknowledgement that it was agonising to be trying to rescue an animal we have come to know and know by name and yet face obstacles at every turn. I suppose this is why there is so much suffering on this planet. People do not want to become involved and make all sorts of excuses and justifications to avoid putting themselves out.

We continued to drive by. We were going to the kennels every Sunday and this presented us with another day and chance where we could try and see him. I sent mum mad by insisting that we must go past Will on the way home. We once saw the older son, but there was never any sign of Will. However, we started to realise that more and more windows were smashed and boarded. It was insane. We were never going to see Will again. I made another report to the inspector in the hope that some action would be taken. I am sure that she was sick of the sound of my voice, but it was the only option available to me. I hoped Will was out of his misery. Harsh as it sounds and felt, it was perhaps the best and only way for him. I did not want him to be suffering.

Meanwhile, we continued at the kennels. Storm and Fleck were as gentle and wonderful as ever. Fleck gave Storm confidence and he would now go to the front door every time if the door bell rang. We were also walking our friends' dogs – a border collie called Mabel, and a sandy coloured mongrel called Stanley. Their owner was very ill and we had met both through the dogs and because I had attended the same school as her son. Stanley was exceptionally strong on the lead and we would be dragged to the forest with Mabel pulling too in order to keep up! Mabel was fantastic fun! She would find the most gigantic of logs and carry them around the forest with her, dropping them at our feet and insisting we throw these tree-like specimens for her to fetch! She would put them down, run on and turn round, bottom in the air in anticipation and with her one blue eye looking intently at us ready for the awaited throw!

Apart from Will, we were not used to barking dogs or dogs that pull as the greyhounds are so gentle! Both Stanley and Mabel could be let off the lead once in the forest and Fleck would charge around with them, enjoying her freedom and splashing through puddles! Stan would attempt to eat anything and everything so when we first gave out treats, it was rather a shock to nearly lose my hand in the process! The greyhounds take treats from your hand with such gentile refinement, accepting them graciously and gently. Stan would chomp at the treat in his enthusiasm and grab it like a thug from your hand without realising that your arm was still attached! Mabel was more ladylike and would come and sit without command to accept her gravy bone. Storm very rarely took treats outside the home, so his portion was duly divided between Stanley, Mabel and Fleck.

At the kennels, Fleck's daughter, Lady, had come in. I was desperate to reunite 'ma Fleck' with her little Lady, but mum was not having it, partly saying 'no' due to the necessity of keeping a space available for Will. When I rang mum from the kennels to ask if we could have Lady, she was visiting our friend, Brenda, the owner of Stanley and Mabel.

Despite her illness, she had a good sense of humour and enjoyed a good laugh at the apoplectic state which was mum's reaction to the request to bring in a third dog, potentially meaning four dogs if we could get Will out! Surely we could have Lady and Will? What would be wrong with walking six dogs? I could not understand the problem!!

It wasn't going to happen though. We were not going to get Will out as all efforts to get him back were coming to nothing. I had to keep thinking though as I could not rest until I could get him out.

One Sunday, we had a visit at the kennels from a family looking to adopt a greyhound. This was always an exciting event as the prospect of a dog getting a lovely home is always the best part of working with rescued animals. I asked them about their lifestyle and the sort of home they can offer the dog. This helps us to ensure they are responsible owners as well as helping us match the dog with the family. There is no point in just picking out any dog as the dog will simply come back and a home be lost. It is crucial to get the right dog in the right home. During the course of the conversation, I asked them where they lived. They lived in Will's area so I took the opportunity to question whether they had ever seen a brindle greyhound walking around in the area. They shook their heads. They were not aware of him and had never seen him. For the sake of the homecheck, I asked them where exactly they lived in the area. They gave me the number of the house and the next few words led me to request they repeat the name of their road. It was Will's road. I tried to calculate in my head whether they were near Will, but the road was confusing as the numbers on one side of the street did not quite tally with the numbers on the other, meaning one could get a false impression that houses were near to each other when in actual fact they were at opposite ends of a very long road. I worked out in my head that the number was nowhere near to Will. What a disappointment as they would probably therefore be even less likely to know about his existence or plight. They had already stated they were not aware of a brindle greyhound anyway. Suddenly, however, it twigged. They were not at the other end of the street as I had initially thought, they were just a few doors away from Will!

43

It was unbelievable. Had I struck gold at last? Would this family, who had just walked through the gate unexpectedly, be able to put my mind at rest that sending Will back into his home had not been so bad after all? I had to ask again.

"Do you ever see the greyhound near you?"... I explained the property where I knew Will lived and gave them the number.

"There are no dogs in that house," came the response.

What? All my hopes were dashed in that single sentence. Once again, my heart crumpled and despite usually priding myself on remaining level-headed, I could not stop myself dissolving into tears despite my futile attempts to control myself and my prolific apologies that I was in such a state. I felt very silly for crying, but the feelings of desolation of now not even knowing where Will was, were all consuming.

"You are not going to give them a dog are you?... Don't ever let a dog go there".

This did a lot to stop my anguish didn't it! It just served to underline and emphasise all the worries and anxieties I knew were true, but that I had tried to push beneath the surface in order to carry on. It was devastating to hear it in such plain terms and with no caveats to soften the blow.

They were convinced that there were no dogs in the house. They said that they would do their best to talk to the occupants and see what had happened to the greyhound. They said there was drug dealing going on and people going in and out of the house with Staffie dogs at all times of the day and night. This was terrible. If Will was there, what was he going through? Was he being fed if people there were in a drug induced stupor? Were they using the Staffie's for illegal cruel activities, such as was going on in Afghanistan, with Will caught in the middle?

Staffie's are such wonderful dogs and have been sadly taken on as the dog of choice for people who want to use them as a status symbol, usually on street corners to make them look macho. As Paul O'Grady points out in his book "The Savage Years", the Staffie used to be the nanny dog, employed to care for children due to its characteristic gentleness. It is an absolute travesty that this dog has been overbred and exploited in such vast numbers that as I write, rescue centres are full to bursting with this breed and hundreds of Staffordshire Bull Terriers are destroyed every year as not enough homes are available. Ridiculously, these dogs continue to be bred prolonging the absurdity of more homes becoming necessary when the next batch of unwanted puppies, if they are lucky, eventually make it to a rescue centre or end up discarded like an old sofa.

Was Will suffering violence as a punch-bag himself? Did he have water in the height of the hot weather or a warm place to sleep when it was cold? I knew I would never see him again. If he wasn't there, where was he? Why was it so difficult to give a needy dog a good life and get him away from a situation in which everybody was confirming was no place for any creature?

I continued to drive past just in case they were wrong, though it was clearly even less likely that I would catch a glimpse of him or something that might reassure me that he was ok. After the encounter with the neighbours, I came home and rang the helpline again to speak to the inspector. I knew the organisation did not want to go in again, but they were the only ones with the authority to act so I had to turn to them.

"What's the latest?" asked the inspector when she rang.

I relayed the story and it was all a revelation to the inspector. I had no more information as the call with further details from the neighbours had not materialised. The inspector promised to call if she heard any more and again I resigned myself to a long and fruitless wait.

What else could I do to get him out? I was not going to do anything illegal as it should be possible to do the right thing lawfully in a country with animal protection laws; and going against the law would not help in the long run. One person I know had suggested that we storm the house, break the door down, grab the dog and do a runner with him.

But this would not solve anything and people could get seriously hurt. Surely there had to be a more reasonable way. I greatly admire those who fight the law and who sometimes tread the boundary of the law for the sake of the right and the good, but on this occasion there was nothing more I could do than hope my persistence would pay off in the end. I was not optimistic, but just maybe, if I kept pushing, kept offering the dog a home so he would not cost anyone any money, and kept hassling, it would result in it becoming easier for them to get the poor creature out. Having worked for a charity, an apparent altruistic concern, I was not naive enough to realise that it would be better to get them to realise that they would benefit and get a more peaceful life rather than me raising concerns about the actual welfare needs of the dog. Sad, but true.

After about four weeks with no news and no sign of anything, surprisingly, I was shocked to receive a phone call. The inspector had been called to the home after reports of a Staffie dog being hit with a belt in the park. The phone call informed me that the greyhound was 'still in the house' and that the family also had a Staffie who was playing with a ball. It was said that while both looked thin, they were 'ok'. But what does 'ok' mean? If it is simply that they are not dead, then that is not good enough in my book. Every animal deserves no less than a kind and loving home.

So it was clear that the family who had visited the kennels had never seen Will and did not even know of his existence. This must mean he was never walked and never seen out of the house. At least I knew he was still in the house.

As the months had passed, I was beginning to react in a split way. Part of me was still very upset by the potential cruelty that Will was going through. The other part of me was numbed by it and resigned to the next piece of bad news about him. I would swing like a barometer between these two extremes which would at times leave me very upset and, at other times, allow me, for a few hours, to block out what was going on. I was also aware that nobody had the will or determination to remove him and return him to me. I had lost hope in the system and just clung to the thought that maybe one day he would somehow find his own way back to me.

It is so deflating and demoralising that despite your best efforts and exhausting every avenue, those who could and should act to defend the defenceless do not feel the same.

More calls and emails followed. I tried other organisations, other rescue places and individuals for tips and advice on what to do and where to go, but everything was hopeless. There are so many animals needing help that people had enough on their hands with the dogs they knew about.

The months rolled on and I still did not have any news. Phone call after phone call was made and detours via the house continued with me varying the time of day as often as I could, going by at weekends, late at night, early in the morning and at all sorts of different hours of the day. There was never any sign of Will. We once went to dinner with some friends who lived nearby and decided to drive home a different way in order to go past Will. On this occasion, we saw lights on in the bedroom with two shadowy figures in the window, but this told us nothing. The house was very distinguishable with its broken windows and unpainted woodwork.

I tried to do some research into the house, but all google searches and attempts to find out information also came to nothing. The only exception to this was when I typed in the number of the house and the road accompanied by the word 'dog'. I was horrified to uncover a posting by someone in the local vicinity who had typed a message on a website outlining how worried he was because two dogs were being kept out in the snow at this address. The weather outside had turned bitterly cold with heavy snow causing chaos on the roads. How could any dog survive outside in such conditions? This small segment confirmed what we had feared. It also reiterated that there was a Staffie living with Will. It was heart wrenching to read this post and know I was powerless to help. This was so unnecessary as a warm bed was sitting in the garage. I am not normally childish about these things, but for some reason, I could not bear to look at the green bed that Will had used during his brief stay with us. It just triggered memories of him and what he must be enduring. So it was packed away and stored in the garage.

I was throwing myself into helping out more at the kennels. If I could help these dogs at least I could do something, however small, to make their lives more tolerable and help them find loving homes. I could not help but sometimes look into the end kennel and at the bars where Will had sat waiting for us to finish our work and go home. He had put his feet on those bars at the door and looked out as we walked by. It was just agonising to not know what was happening to him.

Chapter 5:

"The whole village is out looking for the Greyhound"

Life at the rescue kennels continued with the usual ups and downs. Each dog that came into its care had a story of its own and some ended up with an extension to that story once in our hands!

It is always the highlight of any day or week to see a dog go off to a new home when you know they are going with lovely people and will be loved and cared for. Of course, there is the element of frustration that the process has not ended because no sooner as one dog goes home, there are endless numbers waiting to come in. However, helping one dog, actually helps two dogs as another dog can find a space in the rescue kennels. This goes back to my persistent gripe that breeding regulations must be introduced as currently the situation is absurd.

However, at least when they have reached the rescue kennels, they have run the gauntlet and made it to a place of security. It is then our responsibility to ensure they go to loving homes. All homes are checked and re-checked because we do get a range of people coming through the gates! We have to make sure the dog is going to the right home for that dog and that the people will treat them as a loved member of the family. Sometimes, of course, a home does not work out and we always insist the dog comes back to us as the kennels is its second home and we are there to safeguard the welfare of the dog from cradle to grave. It is always upsetting to see a dog come back after having a home, but the consolation is that the dog is, at least, coming back and not disappearing somewhere else. Of course, there are genuine reasons, but sometimes (and quite frequently) people do make up excuses to justify why they are returning the dog. The usual reasons are a new baby, marriage break-up, the dog is suddenly urinating indoors (after six years), when really the family no longer wants the responsibility of owning the dog. It is much better to be honest, rather than label the dog, as we have more respect for honesty and it helps the dog to find a new home much more easily. If a dog becomes saddled with an unwarranted reputation it can hamper its chances of being re-

49

homed again quickly because we have to bear the comments in mind in case the description from the previous owner is accurate. Ultimately, making things up is daft and makes the returner look more foolish, as when the dog is re-homed, we often get the truth anyway!

Dolly was one dog who we home-checked that was sadly returned to the kennels through no fault of her own. She had gone to a family who lived nearby and they had claimed she was suddenly urinating in the house. Dolly was lucky enough to be chosen (along with another dog called, Stan) to find a home with a long-term adopter who was emigrating to Malta and taking the dogs with her. It took six months for the relevant paperwork and veterinary procedures to be carried out, but they then set off for Malta! The owner had hired a car to transport them through France and Italy where they would board a ferry for the long journey to Malta! The ferry was very dog-friendly and the dogs could share the cabin with their new owner! It was good that Stan and Dolly were together as they had shared a kennel for six months so had established a secure bond which would help them on the journey. What a wonderful life they now lead – running on the beaches and lazing on the patio of a villa in the sun. It is rather different to living on the outskirts of a town for Dolly! Perhaps she should send a postcard to her previous owners as she has been clean in her new home!

These dogs know such a variety of homes. It is strange to think that some have acres of land while others live in flats. Some go five minutes down the road to a home in the local area whilst others live in the country or the city and experience things of which some human beings can only dream. The life they will know will differ so much from dog to dog and it is the luck of the moment and who will experience a particular set of circumstances when a visiting adopter makes their selection. However, as long as the dog is loved and cared for, this is the main requirement. As far as I am concerned, the adopter could live in a shed if they give the dog a loving home!

Meanwhile, Little Lady, so precious to me as Fleck's daughter, had been tried out by one of the volunteers, but sadly it had not worked out.

They had two other greyhounds and Lady had had a bit of diarrhoea when she first went home. The advice had been to starve her to clear the bug but unfortunately, she had seen the other dogs eating and become frustrated and agitated. She then went to live with a small dog, but was returned from this home too. She had come back to kennels with a mysterious wound on her front leg which had really subdued her. We did not get to the root cause of this wound, but it may have been a bite from the other dog. She was such a playful girl normally, once grabbing my Wellington Boot in play whilst out in the paddock and wrestling with my foot! She had been wagging her tail like mad as I hopped around in a vain attempt to regain my Wellie! She was a real comedian of a dog who loved a cuddle and had a real sense of fun! Lady really needed a loving home now she was back, yet again, in kennels. She was starting to get labelled when, as I said above, it is better for people to admit that they should not have taken on the extra responsibility in the first place rather than bring the dog back accompanied by lame excuses which say more about the inadequacies of the humans' commitment than the actual behaviour of the dog. Again, this is not to dismiss the valid reasons for returning a dog, but honesty is the best policy! Mum was still not caving into pressure though!

Thankfully, Lady's next option was a wonderful home in which she is idolised and utterly adored. Her past trauma had made her a bit unsettled and, unusually for greyhounds, she had been prone to barking when left alone. Normally greyhounds do not bark once they go home, but I suppose there is always the exception that proves the rule! Through persistence and love, Lady and her new owner overcame these difficulties and she is doted upon as all greyhounds should be! It is rather nice as I still get to see her too! She really takes after her mum too. It is comical to witness how both Fleck and Lady possess the quality of seeing the fun in situations! It was a fantastic result for Lady. I could not have her so she was in the best possible home.

Meanwhile, other dogs were continuing to come and go at the kennels. All sorts of homes continued to need checking and we were sometimes fascinated by the diverse and very varied places we visited. We met some lovely people, but also had to turn down a few worrying homes. One couple seemed to think they could have a greyhound as an alternative to a burglar alarm. I pointed out that they would be more likely to welcome the intruder, hold the door open whilst the TV was stolen and help load it into the van! Another home thought they could use the greyhound as a running companion. Despite the greyhound's athletic racing career, this is not an option. They are sprinters, not able to do distances; and long distances at speed would, quite literally, do them serious damage, if not kill them as they cannot physically cope with it.

On occasions, a team of us have been deployed on bizarre rescue missions which could be a book in themselves!

Mandy

The recovery of Mandy was one of the most amazing missions we have had to undertake for the welfare of these greyhounds! Mandy had been re-homed to a goat-farm in a rural location. Mandy was a very nervous greyhound when she came into the kennels. She would go out into the paddocks and we would often spend most of the rest of the day trying to get her back in! She would come towards us and then scoot off in another direction, just as you were about to throw the slip-lead around her neck. In the end, we had to barricade an alleyway between the paddocks where we could corner her more easily! Due to her nerves, she had been petrified of cats and other animals. Being 'cat-friendly', she was likely to find a home more quickly and her chance had come when the family with the goats (and several cats!) had visited looking for a dog.

Unfortunately, the new owners had clearly not heeded our warnings that greyhounds must only initially be let off the lead in a safe and fully enclosed area.

We received an email to say that Mandy was lost and had been missing since the day she had been homed. Winter was fast approaching with heavy snow forecast and stark frozen nights already setting in. There was absolutely no way that she would survive unless she was found. Apparently she had a coat on, but this could become more worrying if it rained and the coat became damp and cold.

After several nights worrying, looking out of the window and imagining what Mandy was going through, (and with no news from the new owners) we travelled there a few days later. An initial scouting of the area made us realise that it was like looking for a needle in a haystack. Sadly the owners were not being proactive and, judging by the surroundings, she was not likely to be picked up as it was so remote and the countryside so vast between towns. She would not stray into neighbourhoods or be easily cornered. Previous experience of catching Mandy in an enclosed space made the prospect of catching her in such a mammoth landscape seem utterly remote. The owner directed us down the road to where Mandy had last been seen; with the comment "she seemed quite happy". Our patience and sympathy was starting to wane as we did not see any posters or any attempt by the new owners to locate Mandy. If their parting words were anything to go on, it was essential that we found her before it was too late. We came across a wooded area which seemed to surround the farm. Perhaps Mandy had gone to ground in the woods somewhere. All sorts of hazards could present themselves in there though. She could get caught on barbed wire, in an animal trap or even get caught on a branch by her collar and choke. We called as loudly as we could, but did not even hear a twig crack. She could have been looking at us for all we knew, staring out from behind a bush before slinking off into the undergrowth. There was a pond from which she could get water, but it also presented a drowning fear. There were fallen trees and undergrowth where she could shelter, but this only underlined the worry that she could become trapped and be unable to free herself. We had no luck that day and the darkness was starting to close in so we called it a day, vowing to come back with a bigger team at the first available opportunity. We also discussed it with the owner of the kennels who suggested we take some dogs with us in the hope that Mandy would go to them if she was too frightened to come to us.

A week after she had been lost, and two days after my mum and I had been looking, a group of us from the kennels set off on a mission to find Mandy. It was a Sunday and the journey to the spot took over an hour. This time we did not inform the owners that we were in the area.

We started in the lane near to the farm and the woods behind, putting up posters as we went, calling and telling everyone we met. Our biggest worries were twofold: would we even see Mandy and how would we catch her if we did see her? Even with the dogs reassuring presence, she had been out for a week and this would only have served to make her even more anxious. Of course, another scenario was that she would be too weak to make herself known; but perhaps this might help our cause if we did come upon her as she would not be so quick to get away.

As the path divided into two, our group split into pairings. We each took our own section of the wood and the neighbouring little village. Three of us went one way accompanied by two dogs; and two of us went the other with another two greyhounds. The locals were all very helpful as word started to spread that there were four greyhounds and five people looking for a missing greyhound! One chap was kindly carrying rope with him in case he saw Mandy! There had been some sightings and gathering the picture of Mandy's movements enabled us to see that she was not sticking in one place, but moving around the countryside, scavenging in the village, and heading back into the countryside, doubling back on areas she had previously covered. The likelihood that we had trodden paths down which she had been was great, but with the increasing realisation that she could also be miles away by now. It was a nightmare as not only could she freeze or starve to death, get entangled in undergrowth, she could also be run over on the roads or shot on farmland.

The village was so small that we were quickly reunited with the rest of our group who appeared from a lane opposite. We parted again and obsessively checked every alleyway and walkway, going into places where she would clearly not be in hiding, just in case there was something we had missed. One member of our team, John, was keeping our spirits up and as we joined him down another lane, he was standing near an outbuilding with his back to us. As we came round the corner, he was deep in conversation.

"Just chatting to one of the locals", he nonchalantly quipped as he stood back to reveal a huge grey horse looking over a stable door!

As we rejoined the main road, one member of the other half of our team was waving frantically on the other side. The other member had been picked up in a car by a local who believed they had seen Mandy that morning.

"So someone has taken my wife in the car?" said our joker... "I might never see her again...". Then came the comedy pause... "I should be so lucky".

We made our way down the road in the general direction and eventually caught up with his wife who had been deposited along the road. She was looking into front gardens, over garden-gates and behind walls! Again we divided, taking different roads. I took Storm down one lane, bordered by houses on one side and woodland on the other. One lady in a car stopped us, took my number and promised to ring if she saw any trace of Mandy.

Everyone was being so kind! Sadly, however, we were not having any success and our poor dogs were already exhausted. It certainly underlined the fact that greyhounds do not like huge amounts of exercise! We were starting to have to encourage them and chivvy them along! We reconvened outside a local pub for a brief respite and to rest the dogs. Two of us decided to walk on a little on our own. It was too much to stand still, however tired we were, as the adrenalin and anxiety of knowing Mandy was out there, meant we just had to keep going. What if Mandy was just two steps further on from where we had decided to go back. We did not get very far, checking a cricket ground on the way, before my mobile rang.

Back at the pub, our distinguishable crew of resting greyhounds and searchers had been approached by a couple who had walked through the fields from their home and had seen Mandy in a field not far from their home in the next town. We mobilised into action again! The couple gave us good directions, but advised it would be quicker to drive to the location. This necessitated a mad dash back to the cars which we had parked about two miles away. It did, however, present a useful opportunity to give the dogs a much needed break (even if they had to walk two miles to achieve it!).

We followed the complicated instructions and parked in a housing estate that backed onto fields and more forest land. We again split into two groups. My pairing which comprised of myself and a volunteer called, Jim, together with Storm and Fleck who were unceremoniously dragged and bribed from the car, went down into the valley and we determined to push on along the muddy path. We battled on, a copse of trees on one side, planted fields on the other. My mobile had been bleeping in protest that it was running out of battery. For the most part, we were so isolated that we did not have any signal so we had no idea where our team-mates were! We must have walked for over an hour when our mobiles rang. Someone in the other village, from where we had just come, had spotted Mandy back by the church near the goat farm at which we had started; and, coming across one of our posters, was calling to let us know! Jim did not have the number of anyone in the other group on his phone and I just managed to text it to him before my phone died completely! This was the start of some of the amazing coincidences that occurred that day! It was remarkable that we had had signal to receive the call in the undulating valley and that we had only just been able to communicate with the other team!

They headed back to the village with their dogs, Skye and Ranger in the car, leaving mum behind in the other vehicle to wait for our return. Storm and Fleck were utterly exhausted and seemed to have gone into robotic mode, placing one foot in front of the other. I made comforting noises as we couldn't stop now. We were so close to Mandy and even though the whole task seemed fruitless, it was certainly not something we put the dogs through on a regular basis and they would just have to keep going somehow! As we turned back to head back to mum and the car, we heard footsteps and voices approaching down the muddy pathway in front of us. Coming back across the valley was the lovely couple who had directed us to the other town. They were so kind and decided to show us where they had seen Mandy earlier in case she headed back in that direction. We stumbled up the path back to an open stretch of grassland where they then offered to walk us across the fields, the quick route (if you knew the way!), back to the village. My poor dogs were losing the will to live, resisting walking another step, but they bravely turned round as we retraced our steps and headed across the fields.

At one point, we thought we had spotted her and my heart started racing. The black dog in the distance was on its own and heading down a furrowed field. We had to do a double-take and check with each other that this was not a mirage as by this stage we were starting to see black dogs in every shadow! We were convinced we had at least seen Mandy and Jim took the high point of the field with Fleck, I went down to the bottom and our new friends walked in the middle. We had every direction covered and the only way she could escape from us was to walk in front of us. As we walked across the field, we were hatching plans of ways in which we could grab her! However, this soon proved unnecessary when a man appeared and put his black Labrador on a lead! We really were seeing things now! We all felt a bit foolish as well as having our hopes dashed! Eventually, having negotiated   several stiles and finding alternative routes which a tall (and weary) greyhound could walk, we reached the church and found a member of our team, but no Mandy.

Darkness had started to set in during our walk and the lights were on in the church. The congregation had started to arrive and the vicar informed us that, "the whole village is out looking for the greyhound"!

It was very cold now too and our hands were blue and our breath creating smoke in front of us. As the gathering gloom descended around us, Storm and Fleck could not walk another step! We were giving up hope. What more could we do!? We had walked for about six hours and could do no more. Storm and Fleck could certainly do no more and were absolutely exhausted. We would not find Mandy now, in the dark. But where was mum? She did not have a mobile with her and was stuck in the dark, in her car back in the other town! It was decided that one of our team would have to drive back to get mum while we waited where we were. It was thought that Skye and Ranger might need to relieve themselves so they got out of the car to wait with us. There was no way that Storm and Fleck were going anywhere else!! Therefore, when it was suggested that we have one final walk into the woods to check for one last time, I stayed in the churchyard with Storm and Fleck; while Skye and Ranger took over the 'dog-attracting' role, having had their rest in the car.

It was so cold, the area was pitch black as the church lights were on around the other side of the building; and apart from the occasional headlight of people arriving for church, I could barely see much around me. Storm and Fleck were whining and I tried to give them reassurance. It wouldn't be long now and we would be back in the car where they could sleep all the way home. We had not found Mandy but we had tried. We would go home and rest and think another day about the next course of action. The woodland behind me was quite intimidating as we stood on our own, mobile-less and waiting. Cracking branches swaying in the wind and rustling leaves would be followed by deathly silences, broken by a hoot or another rustle. The moon appeared from behind a cloud and gave a glow to the black outline of the trees that were starting to blend into one in the increasing and incoming fog. It crossed my mind that I could be in for a long wait. Mum would have to be located and then they would have to make their way back to us. The instructions were complex in the light so how would they fair in the dark? I reassured myself that the others would not be too far away as they would have to make their way back to me from the forest in the dark too.

Suddenly, I was awoken from my thoughts by a flurry of activity around me. Mum was there with John, both sets of headlights glaring through the mist. Out of the gloom, from the other direction, came three dogs, followed by Jim and the other lady who had looked in the woods. I rubbed my eyes and had to look twice! Had they not left me with two dogs? It was Mandy!! Fleck started to wag her tail despite her weariness and she pushed forward to give Mandy a friendly lick and welcome!

It transpired that the group had gone into the woods until the fog had started to descend and the dogs were flagging again. As they had turned to come back to the church, Ranger, one of the dogs, had whimpered. Turning round, Jim had offered encouraging words to him, telling him they were going back. Behind Ranger, Mandy was following! It was a miracle! I gave her a few slices of ham. They had wrapped about five leads around her to be sure she could not escape again! The congregation were continuing to arrive and we were being asked to move forward! We bundled Mandy into the car where she lay on Fleck in the boot. I squeezed into the back with a comatose Storm. Fleck was so wonderful with everything and all three dogs were totally exhausted that they just fell asleep on top of each other!

It was a momentous find and we could not believe the outcome, so late in the day and only due to the coincidence of having to return to fetch mum, combined with the determination to have one last look in the forest. There was no way Mandy was going back to the new owners who had heard of our search and encountered us once throughout that long day. They had dismissed our efforts by saying, "well, she's not up there" as they walked down one lane. Jim offered Mandy a home and we took her straight there so she could rest in the warm and get a good meal inside her. She had lost a lot of weight, was not wearing a coat and did not have her collar or lead on her, suggesting she had not slipped the lead as we had been told, but let off the lead on the first day.

We went over and over the story on the way home, interrupted only by Storm, who kept opening the window by leaning on the electric controls when he rested his head on the door! The intermittent blasts of cold air woke us up and sent us into a frenzy every time, in paranoia that Mandy would leap out and end up somewhere on the motorway! Of course, she was far too tired for that (and probably far too relieved to be back with other dogs and safe again), but when we eventually arrived at Jim's house, we took no chances when it came to getting her out of the car. I held the excessive amount of leads from the back and passed them out to mum and Jim as we opened the boot of the car to ensure there was absolutely no risk of her flying off again!

We dined out on this story for months, boring everyone to tears in the process! It was just so amazing that she had been found at such a late hour and when we had more or less given up!

Ranger

Not long afterwards, one of the volunteers' own dogs went missing after being let off the lead in an enclosed area that turned out to have a hole in the fence. The dog, also called Ranger, had run out of the park and disappeared. Sightings had placed him on the other side of a busy A-road. A similar trek across the countryside ensued. This time, we did not put our dogs through so much hiking, but went around in the car to various points and gave them much more rest in between.

At one point we tried to cross a field in which three horses were grazing, oblivious to the greyhound search that was underway. One of them did not take too kindly to the invasion of their field and started coming towards us with a meaningful expression on his face. We took off back to the gate as fast as our (human) legs could carry us! Again, it was a vast area to search, but it was slightly more populated, meaning we hoped Ranger would be picked up by someone if we did not find him. However, again, we had the fear of him being shot on farmland or run down on the roads. There were quite a lot of game-birds around too meaning we must be in a shooting area. This supposed sport means that the birds are likely to be protected by snares which trap and kill wild predators which might harm the birds. These vile and archaic contraptions cause immense suffering to our wildlife and posed a further risk to Ranger. We tramped around across the countryside with the dogs and drove around the area repeatedly, going down the same roads in case Ranger had 'done a Mandy' and recovered the same ground.

Thankfully, although we had no success with his recovery, Ranger was later found on the outskirts of the area in which we had searched, walking along a main road and jumping into a car that had stopped to help him. It was another big relief. The thought of them being alone and frightened, cold and hungry is so difficult to bear and you just want to be out and about until they are recovered.

There are some lovely homes and the majority of adopters are lovely people who offer the dogs new lives, but sometimes human behaviour leaves you cold. Another case involved us having to take back a dog from a home after the man of the family openly spoke about "hating the dog". The dog was absolutely petrified of him. A friend of mine, who coincidentally had the same surname as the dog in question, managed to find him a lovely home with a friend of hers so thankfully, it was a happy ending.

Then there was another dog, Gus, whose owner had wanted to put him down after putting him through countless medical tests and veterinary treatments. It has been suggested to us that his previous owner may have had a version of Munchausen By Proxy – a disease in which medical tests are continually sought regardless of any presence of illness. He has a wonderful home now; and it was discovered that he has absolutely nothing wrong with him, except this history having left him with a terrible fear of vets.

Other dogs are returned after years in a home; and while most are in a reasonable condition when initially brought to the kennels, some come in a very nervous state or needing baths to remove fleas and dirt. One, a male called Jake, was another favourite of mine who was very defensive, but so loving once you won his trust. He now has a wonderful home too. You really do see both extremes of humanity.

Meanwhile, I was making calls to any organisation and any authority that I could think of that might help with Will. I continued to drive past the house, but did not ever see him. I spoke to people involved with Health and Safety about the state of the house and garden, but again, someone directly affected had to call before any action could be taken. I also spoke to several animal rescuers involved in small rescue organisations who offered their support but could not do anything to get Will out.

Lily

Another rescue mission came in the form of having to take a dog from her home after the owner wanted to return her, but had not turned up. Four of us met at the kennels and travelled up to the home with the threat (again) of oncoming snow and had to engage in negotiation on the doorstep with a bitter wind howling in our faces. The owner had changed her mind and became quite hostile when we asked her for the dog. It soon transpired, however, that a change of partner since the adoption of Lily had caused the dog to be kept in the garden. The new partner was also defensive, until he realised that we had no gripe with the family and just wanted to safeguard the welfare of the dog. Greyhounds should never be kept in the garden. They cannot deal with cold or hot temperatures and need somewhere inside that is safe and warm. Moreover, these dogs have come to us to find loving homes and not to be kept outside. It was utterly freezing and for some reason, I did not think we would leave without the dog. I was not going anywhere until I had Lily in the car and on the way to the new home that was ready and waiting for her.

After much negotiation and exchange of views, it was finally agreed that Lily could come with us. We hurriedly put her in the car and made the journey back to the kennels to pick up the other car. On the way, the snow descended and we were so relieved and thankful that Lily was not out in the garden to freeze to death that night. Instead, we deposited her with a lovely caring lady who took her in, gave her a lovely warm bed and some roast chicken that she had especially prepared for her arrival. Lily was also quite thin, quite elderly at ten years old and yet so gentle and still wagged her tail. When she arrived at her new home, she even asked to go out to go to the toilet. She was no trouble at all and it was an absolute travesty that the previous owners had abused her trust in this way.

A little while later, when the weather had warmed a little, we had a third missing greyhound on our hands! This never happens, but I guess things come in threes! One of the dogs from the kennels, Sally, who had a home, but who we knew well through regular visits had slipped her lead. This time, she was missing in a heavily built-up and congested area. The fears were therefore different, although with the same threat of danger from roads. Mainly, however, the worry was: who would pick her up? Could she fall into the wrong hands?

A group of us, many including those who had found Mandy gathered again. We were becoming used to this! We walked the streets and parks again, picking places we assumed a greyhound would hide. Sadly, we did not have any luck but we also popped into the local pet store chain and reported her as missing. It was useful to know they have a lost/found book. I also determined to ring the wardens of all the local boroughs. Since Will, we had learnt that councils do not liaise. I was reminded that if a dog crosses the border into another neighbouring borough, there is no legal obligation to inform other councils that dogs are lost or found. Therefore, unless the owner rings every borough in the vicinity, the dog could be picked up, but remain unclaimed. This means seven days before the dog is put to sleep or re-homed. It is a daft situation and money could be saved if there was a central database of missing and picked up dogs.

Anyway, I now had the number, name and email address of the manager of the dog enforcement team of my neighbouring borough; Will's borough.

Thankfully, Sally was found, brought into the council and returned to her owners. We will never know where she slept, but at least she was safe and well.

Dandy

Another incident involved a dog called Dandy, who had been at the kennels for over two years. One volunteer had taken a liking to Dandy and offered to foster him. He then decided to keep him, but we had to do a follow-up home-check.

When we arrived, he had forgotten we were coming, but we gave him the benefit of the doubt when we saw Dandy happily curled up on the floor in a comfortable bed surrounded by toys. He certainly doted upon him and seemed very happy to have him in his family. Whether his wife was equally as happy is debatable and, particularly since our experiences with the dog who was 'hated' by the husband, we know that it is always crucial to establish that the whole family agrees that having a dog is desirable.

We set out how important it was to keep Dandy on the lead and not take any chances until you know how he will react to other dogs. He seemed to take this on board. However, the following day, we learnt that his son had taken Dandy to the park and, thinking it was 'cool' to run with a 40mph sprinter, had let him off the lead. Dandy had taken off out of the park, but at that moment it was unclear in which direction he had headed. One way would take him towards a busy motorway; other ways would lead him in several directions towards towns or along a river. Another nightmare was starting to unfold.

Again we phoned every local council and informed all the vets in the area. It happened to be a weekend so messages were left with councils, rather than the dog wardens themselves. We scouted around the area in the car again, not having a clue where to start this search. After driving around for a while, a call came through on my mobile from the owner of the kennels. Dandy had been picked up very near to where I live! He had actually run across my road and caused chaos at the bottom near the main road. He could have caused a serious accident so it was sheer luck that he ended up being picked up safely and was being looked after five minutes from my house by a kind family who had taken him in. They had rung the council who had called the kennel owner. We went to collect him and he wagged his tail and responded to his name. We took him straight back to the kennel where he was taken in and given a nice dinner. Thankfully, some long-term adopters who had originally had to make a choice between Dandy and Charley when looking for a dog, coincidentally rang to ask if Dandy was still at the kennels. They had felt unnecessarily guilty for not choosing Dandy and were now in a position to offer him a home along with Charley and their other dog. It was a wonderful outcome for Dandy who certainly struck gold that day when he found his home with them. Funnily enough, if he had not 'done a runner' he would not have had such a special home and would probably have been returned to the kennels at a later date, having lost his chance at that home.

Having the dogs out loose is an emotional rollercoaster and all consuming. The 'unknown' is the worst aspect and their vulnerability makes focusing on other things very difficult. It helps to get out and look because at least you feel you are doing something, however small, to try and help a dog in need; particularly a dog you know personally.

There was one dog I knew very personally, however, that I was still getting nowhere with. I knew the likelihood was that I would never see Will again, but only I could help him and I just could not stop trying as his suffering would never be guaranteed to end if I abandoned him totally. However, despite all my emails, letters and phone calls, it was getting near to a year and a half having passed since I had even laid eyes on him.

Chapter Six:

"I'll call him Tommy"

Kennel life continued with some lovely homes for more lucky dogs. Four dogs came in one day called Magic, Trainer, Rosie and Ally. Rosie was a beautiful brindle girl who found a home very quickly. Magic was reserved soon afterwards, but tragically he developed a mystical illness a week before we were due to take him to his new home. Usually people come to the kennels to take the dogs home, but occasionally we do deliver the dog if the person is really struggling to find transport. Magic, a black dog, had been offered a lovely home with a very kind young lady who had seen him on the website and felt sorry for his grey face. She had worried that he would be overlooked, being slightly grey and older so had said she would adopt him. Magic started to go downhill, seemingly unable to stand and losing balance. We rushed him to the vet and after many tests, nothing could be done for him. To lose him so close to him finding a lovely home, and after he had spent all his life in kennels, was devastating. Having to take him to the vet was very difficult, knowing that he might not come back again; and yet, he was in pain and it was the kindest thing for him. Losing the dogs is always traumatic and agonising. The dogs at the kennels are safe there and none are ever put down unless it is in the best interest of the dog for health reasons. Thankfully, this situation does not occur too frequently, but when it does happen, it is very sad to deal with and we always remember each individual very clearly.

The most painful of these situations was having to take a black, six year old dog called, Bill, down to the vet to be put to sleep. Bill had been losing weight rapidly and been suffering from ongoing and unending diarrhoea. Despite tests and antibiotics and a trial with treatment for a condition called EPI, a strange illness where the body cannot absorb food despite a ravenous appetite, Bill made no improvement. He was wearing two coats at night as the temperature outside was plummeting. He was still standing, but his body was so painfully thin and skeletal that it was pitiful to see him. In the end, he was refusing food and did not want to come out of his kennel. He was desperately ill and the decision had to be made. The worst part of this process was that we had to wait for the appointment, having been due to go home and realising we could not leave him any longer. We arranged the time with the vet and made the journey in the dark with Bill in the back, knowing he would not set foot in the kennels again. It was heart-breaking and we felt terrible, but we also knew he would be set-free from suffering. Even when at the vet, we had to wait which was even more unbearable. Other dogs were coming in and out and even to the end, Bill had never lost his 'chase' instinct. Most greyhounds will sniff other dogs and be fine, but a few continue to think small breeds are rabbits which they are expected to chase. Bill had been with us a while because of this and it was so sad to know he would never experience the love of a happy home. When we were called in and the vet peeled back his coats, his body was utterly emaciated, despite our best efforts, and as he sank to the floor, we knew we had made the right decision for Bill, however devastating it was for us.

We drove back to the kennels in silence and the fog and cold was closing in around us. It echoed our mood as we came up the hill, before suddenly, in front of us, we came upon a group of four cows meandering down the lane. This wasn't normal! They didn't seem to be accompanied by anyone so we drove on, not knowing what to do and intending to call the RSPCA when we got back to the kennels. As we neared our destination, we came upon two people who were looking for four members of their escaped herd! We could picture Bill, looking down, hopefully having a good laugh at this latest rescue mission! Bill was now free from pain, out of the icy cold and running with his other kennel-friends, who had also known and been part of life at the kennels.

But back to the four arrivals! Magic's potential owner had not met him so was happy to offer a home to another needy dog. Ally had just been down to the vet to have a dental. We had needed gas masks to walk near his kennel as his breath had been absolutely shocking, but after a dental (and the removal of the majority of his teeth), he now had fresh breath and was ready for his new home.

This left Trainer, a lovely black and white dog who was very affectionate and loved a cuddle. He was with us for a while as he was six years old so slightly older than most adopters preferred. One day, we were asked to do a homecheck for a home that happened to be ten minutes from Will. After the check, we took the lady to the kennels to choose a dog as she did not drive. Out walked the black and white dog with his wonderful affectionate and gentle personality. She took to him immediately and would take him home after he was neutered. On the way home, she said, "I'll call him Tommy". This was a vast improvement on 'Trainer'!

His new owner would have to bring Tommy into the kennels a few days a month as she needed to visit her mum who wasn't well at the time. Obviously this presented a problem with the woman's lack of driving capability, so mum volunteered me to run him back and forth each time.

Each time I picked him up, my most direct route to the kennels was past Will's front door. Time and again I drove by, with or without Tommy, in the hope of seeing Will, some sign of him, or something positive from the house, but there was never anything to see.

The months were passing by and I wrote more letters to those who might help; sometimes changing my name in the hope that more pressure would help this poor dog. Perhaps if they didn't recognise my name, they would realise that there really was an animal in serious distress and it wasn't some nutter with nothing better to do. All I wanted was to get Will out of a horrifying situation in which we had been told that he was suffering hunger and abuse.

One month, in April, I was on my way back home with Tommy. As I drove down Will's road, I knew it was pointless to look at the house. It had never revealed anything before so why should it be any different this time? I resigned myself to another look which would lead me nowhere.

The traffic was quite slow, always a bonus for trying to look left while driving! As I neared the house, a bus was coming the other way and I had to pull into a space to let it pass. This enabled me to pull away slowly and I was still going slowly as I drew level with the house. It was very easy to identify as a hedge to the left sandwiched the property between another house with easily distinguishable curtains. The house itself was still in a terrible state, as it had been when we originally put Will back in. All the windows were smashed with holes and jagged glass was covered by pieces of cardboard.

As I drove by, I glanced left, expecting to see the usual closed door and quiet insignificant detail which betrayed nothing of what was going on inside. On this occasion, I did a double-take, however. The door was open and the stairs were visible. There was no carpet – the place looked deserted. I felt a sudden rush of trepidation. Where was Will? Was he loose? Was he in the house, but abandoned? If he wasn't in the house, where on earth was he now? Panic, hope, frustration and anticipation were welling up inside me. But I couldn't stop! It was a busy road and I had Tommy with me, on his way home, in the back of the car!

I decided to take Tommy home and then see what I could do. Perhaps I had imagined it; what could I do anyway – I had exhausted all my ideas, contacts and plans of action. In a state of resigned calm, I dropped off Tommy and decided to drive back past Will's house. As I approached, a sense of dread, combined with expectation was making my heart pound and my mouth go dry. What would I do if I saw something? I would just have to see what happened. Anything I planned would not go seamlessly anyway as events rarely unfold in the way you anticipate!

As I came down the road, I could see that the door was still open. So no one had been going in and out, temporarily leaving it ajar. It had been left open. What was going on? The house looked wrecked, but empty.

I turned left at the next opportunity and went round the block, enabling me to go past the house again. The door was still open. Where was Will?

I drove home, trying to think what to do. I had to go back again. There was no way I was going to rest with what had been the most significant development to date. When I got home, mum was gardening. I convinced her to come back with me immediately.

As we neared the house for the fourth time that day, we had a feeling of impending doom. It was now dawning on me that if he was there, where were the owners; and if he wasn't there, where was he? At least we had known where he was up until this point. But now he might even be worse off than he was before. Alternatively, he may have found a nice home, but what if he had not? Was he suffering somewhere else now; somewhere we could never find him? All sorts of thoughts and questions were filling my head as I battled to stay calm and try to deal logically with the situation in hand.

The door to the house was still open so we pulled into the nearest parking space and started asking along the street. Frustratingly, the first few doors at which we knocked were not answered and all the neighbours were out. One door was opened an inch by a young boy, but he told us that we would have to ask elsewhere. This was ridiculous, surely we could get somewhere now!? Will's house was totally empty and it was clear it had been vacated, probably at speed.

After a lot of walking, knocking and asking, we eventually found a lady who told us a bit more information. The family had been evicted after eighteen months of living hell and a battle to get rid of them. The children had been taken into care and there had been drug dealing, stabbings and all sorts of crime occurring in the house. The family had moved out and taken a Staffordshire Bull Terrier with them. This must have been the dog we knew about that had been seen being hit with a belt in the park and subsequently been seen playing with a ball with Will in the house. We were told that squatters had been living in the house simultaneously with the family and that the squatters had taken the greyhound. Now what were we going to do? There was absolutely no way I was going to find him now; and I wouldn't even have a clue where to start looking.

The nightmare scenario for our poor Will continued to be brought to light. We had been right to be worried. Will had not been fed properly, once being so hungry that he had jumped the fence, looking for food. He had been left out in the garden in all weathers, thus confirming my findings from the internet. Apparently, he had been a lovely, beautiful and friendly dog, but the family had made him defensive and, according to this lady, he was liable to be sometimes aggressive. She had also been worried and reported it, but nothing had been achieved in helping Will.

That numb feeling was sweeping over me once again, and again I was resigned to knowing I was powerless to help a dog I knew was suffering. It was like being defeated over and over with a glimmer of possible progress dashed on every occasion. I would just have to hope that, just maybe, the squatters would love him, or at least care for him more than he had been previously. Sometimes, people who, from their lifestyles would be expected to be harsh, can often be the most caring people with a real acknowledgement of certain compassionate values. But, of course, there was also a niggle that he might be worse off. Was it possible that he could be worse off? What if he was in even worse hands? The possibilities did not bear thinking about. But I was unable to do anything.

These developments had happened a day before mum was due to go into hospital to have a hip replacement. She had been busy doing the garden in preparation, knowing that she would not be able to do it for a long while. The timing could not really have been worse. I wanted to go on every website to see if any dogs in rescue centres matched Will's description, I wanted to drive round the local area and see if I could see him, I wanted to just do something. I started to trawl through the most obvious sites and then, without success, I looked through the smaller organisations. However, the scope of the mission was immense and some of the sites may not have yet been updated as I did not know exactly when the family had left the house. Time was ticking on and, with mum to care for, I determined to email as many places as I could think of which may, either now or in the future, come into contact with

Will. It was an unlikely method of finding him, but it was the best I could do. I emailed all the greyhound rescue centres in the area, all the other rescues and the main dog homes, explaining a brief version of the story and asking them to contact me if a dog matching Will's description should materialise. In the unlikely event that he was discovered, I would offer him a home and deal with the consequences of this once we had him. I also contacted the national organisation with which I had previously been in contact. It transpired that the lady I had been dealing with had transferred roles and her replacement did not know I would have adopted Will if they had ever got him out. This angered me as a loving home was available for him and yet, if he had been rescued, I would never have known. Even worse, he may have been put to sleep and again, I would never have known.

I also emailed all the local councils, also giving them a brief version of the story, but offering to help with any greyhounds, using my capacity as a representative of the kennels. Again, I would deal with any consequences at a later date, should they get in touch and need our help. I knew that nothing would come of this, but at least I was doing something and widening the range of those who might come to Will's aid.

Mum went into hospital and the search for Will was put on hold. Realistically, of course, there was not much more I could do. I did not have any idea where he was or even if he was still alive. As I travelled up to see mum each day, I could not help but wonder if Will was being held in any of the houses I went past. From mum's hospital window, I could see a park and a spaniel playing with a ball. Where was Will? If I thought too much about it, I could get very upset, but it was always an underlying worry that would, at times, come charging to the forefront of my brain during quiet moments on the train or when seeing a dog with its owner. In the past, it would even break forth when I was out, potentially about to enjoy myself and being jolted into remembering that Will was out there somewhere. Frustration boiled over at times too. He wasn't wanted by his owner now so why had they not let him go and given him to us two years ago? Now he was missing and I would never know where he had ended up.

Mum had been in hospital for three days when a déjà-vu experience occurred! I had been to the kennels in the morning to do my early shift, but the afternoon was being covered by my colleague to allow me to visit mum. I left the hospital at about 5pm. As I approached the station to take the five stops home, police and transport officials had taped off the entrance and a large queue had formed around the nearest bus stop. Oh dear! This was going to turn into a long slog home. It turned out that someone had thrown a brick at the train and brought the line to a stand-still. I had to get a bus. We were all crammed in like sardines, hardly daring to breathe in case we compressed the person behind us, but eventually we made it to a station. The bus journey had taken so long that the trains were now up and running!!

I finally got home at 6.30pm and let Storm and Fleck into the garden. They had been crossing their legs for longer than I had hoped and were very pleased to get out! What a relief to be home! As they bounced back in, I noticed blood dripping from Fleck's front paw. This was all I needed! She had split her dew claw again and it was hanging off. I needed to take her to the vet or it would be catching and bleeding all night. It was not loose enough for me to just yank off (and nor do I like doing this as it touches my squeamish nerve and isn't too pleasant for the dog either!). Storm would have to stay at home while Fleck and I drove off to the vet. This was a bit reminiscent. I could not help but think that this was the exact position we had been in almost two years ago when the call about Will had come through. Could this be an omen? Would another call come in? It did not of course, but it was a very strange coincidence that this should re-occur given my thoughts had been so frequently with Will recently. Fleck wanted to go home, but first she had to endure a quick cut of the claw, followed by a squeal. This resulted in one bandaged paw and a happier Fleck! She was determined to milk this as much as she could and get as much sympathy as mum now! Her little bandy front legs with huge bandage would be the envy of all her friends at the kennels – the latest fashion in trendy footwear.

Chapter Seven:

"Could you help us with this dog?"

Mum came out of hospital and her recovery continued well at home. As the weeks rolled on, I thought about Will, but knew this was the end of the road. There was no point in driving past the house anymore. He could be somewhere in the borough, but he may have moved to the other end of the country for all I knew. Wherever I went, I might be driving past his house, but I could not know whether or not he was inside.

It was difficult, but I would have to blot it out of my mind. There was nothing more I could do and it was all out of my hands. Dwelling upon it would not help Will and only serve to upset me. However, I was not going to forget about Will either. It is important to remember those who suffer even if you can do nothing to help them. So I thought of him, but had to hope that he was out there somewhere, being looked after; and perhaps, dare I hope, being better cared for with new people.

I did not hold out much hope that any of the contacts I made would get back in touch. With thousands of stray dogs to deal with each year, they would not be looking for Will or think about his case at all. Will had also not been a racing dog so had no distinctive or unique ear-marks to identify him. They probably would not even know it was him even if he did come in. I felt 100% confident that I would know him if I saw him. He has distinctive white socks and was neutered, which, for a stray, can be unusual unless they are a loved pet. He also sits and gives his paw, each one repeatedly, which is not always something greyhounds do.

Six weeks went by. I had heard nothing. Regular searches of the websites of various rescue centres had yielded nothing. It was nothing, nothing, nothing, despite all my efforts. I went online to check my emails repeatedly. Still, nothing.

It had been an early start that day as we had taken a kennel dog to a specialist vet for the removal of a corn (and to be neutered). It had been a long day and I was also quite tired, having had to deal with a couple of issues at the kennels on my return with the dog. When I got home, I went online again to check my emails. The usual junk interspersed a few emails I actually wanted to read, but then an unknown address with the title 'greyhound'. What on earth was this? Probably it was another poor soul that needed rescuing. I didn't recognise the name, but I clicked on the email. Through my weary eyes, it swam into focus that it was from the dog enforcement team at the local council. Thankfully, the man I had dealt with two years ago had left now. This man, Winston, was emailing me because they had kept my name on record as being involved with greyhound rescue and wondered if we could help take in a stray they had picked up.

"Could you help us with this dog?" it said; and continued: "We have picked up a stray greyhound off the streets and he is now in the council pound".

If he wasn't claimed within seven days, he could well end up being put to sleep; unless we could help him.

Winston had attached a photograph of the dog to the email. I idly clicked on the picture. It took a while to open and I wondered what the dog would be like. Hopefully, it would be one that would be easy to home. Perhaps it could even be one of the greyhounds we had homed in the area and we could organise an instant happy reunion with the owner without even having to bring the dog into the kennels. Hopefully, the owner of the kennels would have a space to take him in. I hadn't even asked her yet! The picture appeared on my screen and suddenly I was wide awake. As the picture unfolded before my eyes, I gave a start.... "It's him"....I yelled!

But was it!? The photograph was quite dark and showed a dog behind bars in the pound's kennel. It was a brindle greyhound with white feet. There was a white line across his face. But the photograph was not clear and he was slightly obscured by the bars. I could not see all his

77

feet to compare with the photographs I had taken two years ago. I was shaking now and going cold. I had to know if it was Will, but I also had to reply as quickly as I could so that the council did not put the dog to sleep. I grabbed my photos and frantically tried to find similarities (or even differences). The pound dog had a slightly more chunky head, but one of my photographs of Will showed his head at an angle which could mean this was the same. The dog in the photograph seemed a darker colour than my pictures, but perhaps this could be explained by the shadows in the pound.

I called mum up to the computer. I'm not sure she was as excited, shaken, hopeful or anxious as me! I think she hoped it was a different dog as the imminent arrival of a third dog in the home was hardly filling her with joy.

I replied to the email; shaking, both happy that we may have found Will and with trepidation about what may happen next. Would mum let me keep him? Would Storm accept him this time? Would Will be different after two more years of abuse? What if he had been turned aggressive by all his terrible treatment? But greyhounds are notoriously gentle – so many from the kennels live with babies and children. They are so friendly and loving – it is very rare to see one that you can't trust with the youngest of children. I suppose there could always be an exception which proves the rule though!

The good thing was that we knew he was house-trained. Last time he had been clean, apart from the day following his operation. We also knew he was good with the cats. We had three cats who were comfortable with Storm and Fleck. Will had been fine with them last time. However, we didn't even know if this was Will yet!

My reply made it clear that we would take the dog regardless. "Does he have any distinguishing features", I also asked. "Did he have any ear-marks? Had he been neutered"? "I think it might be the dog I have been looking for for two years", I told them.

I waited on tenterhooks for them to get back to me. I pounced on any email that came through. It had been ten minutes now since I sent it. Come on!! What was the delay?! I had been waiting two years for this! I was at the kennels all day the following day so took the phone number with me. I could not wait all day – I was going mad already!

9am dawned the following morning and I rang the council.

"Welcome to your local council. Please note that calls may be monitored or recorded for training purposes. To enable us to process your enquiry more quickly and help us proceed your request in the best possible way, please choose from one of the following six options: Press one if you know the extension number of the person you are dialling. Press two to make a payment. Press three to enquire about council tax, benefits and school meals. Press four for environment and street services including refuse and recycling, rubbish collection, parking and enviro-crime. Press five for social services, housing and mobility. Press six for all other enquiries".

It must be four.

"Press one for environmental health. Press two for refuse and recycling. Press three for rubbish collection. Press four for parking. Press five for enviro-crime. Press six for all other enquiries".

It must be six.

"Your call has been forwarded to a member of the team, please hold"...

"Your call is important to us, but all members of the team are busy at the moment"...

"Your call is important to us, but you may find the information you require on our website"...

After what seemed like ten years of Greensleaves on loop, I was eventually put through to a human voice.

"I'll put you through to the dog team".

"You have reached the office of the dog enforcement team. We are not at our desks at the moment so please leave a message after the tone".

I left a message and my mobile number wondering why it was so difficult to achieve any progress whenever it came to Will.

After an anxious hour and yet to have a returned call, I rang again. Making it through the automatic rigmarole, I asked the human voice for the extension number of the dog team so that I could put myself through more efficiently. After battling a few more times, I managed to speak to the dog team to try and establish for sure if the dog in the photograph was Will.

"You can go and see him if you like? You could probably take him there and then..."

"Can I come today or tomorrow?"

"I will get back to you before 3pm and let you know the time once I have spoken directly with the kennels".

Of course, I did not hear by the allotted time, so I rang again. I was sure they would be totally sick of me, but I was not going to let this go now!

"I'm sorry, but the person dealing with this dog has gone home for the day. I will get someone to ring you first thing tomorrow".

"Could you just tell me if the dog is neutered? He won't be put to sleep will he because I want to take him off your hands, whether he is the dog I am looking for or not."

"Don't worry, I am the head of the team and nothing can be done without my final say-so".

Well, that was a relief anyway. At least he wasn't in any immediate danger. It was like being on an episode of candid camera though. I was half expecting Dom Joly to appear at any moment and reveal that it had all been a set-up. The frustration was starting to boil over again and it was a good thing I don't drink or I would have ended up in hospital after a mass boozing session to calm the nerves! I just had to know though.

"Could you tell me any more details please?"

"Yes, I can tell you that the 'stray greyhound' was picked up from the streets. He was in the company of a homeless man who flagged down the dog patrol team as our van was passing. He told the team that he had found the dog but did not want him. To be honest with you, he claimed that the dog was not his dog, but the whole team considered that the dog had such a bond with this man that it was actually his dog".

"Sorry to go on and I'm sure you think I'm a real pain, but could you tell me, is the dog neutered? And does he have ear-marks?"

"I can't remember for sure, but I seem to recall that he was neutered and that he did not have any ear-marks".

"So the homeless man does not want him?"

"No, he no longer wanted him. He seemed to have a drink problem too as he had a beer can in one hand and the dog in the other."

I gave my mobile number, my home number, the kennels' number and my email address. I was going to be contactable wherever I was from now on! I did not want to get my hopes up before anything was confirmed, but I had growing anticipation. It seemed to slot into place. The dog looked similar (if not the same), had no ear-marks (unusual if a greyhound), was with a homeless gentleman (which would tie in with squatters being evicted) and was in the same borough.

It was a long night where I continually had to brush away conflicting thoughts that entered my mind. The next day I was also scheduled to be at the kennels, but my mobile was at my side constantly. My big worry now was twofold. First, that it would not be him and then I would have both another dog to worry about and still be no closer to finding Will; and secondly, that messages were not being communicated between the council and the pound. His seven days were nearly up – please don't let them put him down now.

"Is that Louise?"

"Yes... is this regarding the stray greyhound?"

"Yes, this is the council. I understand you wanted to come and see the greyhound?"

"Is this possible? I would love to come and see him. I think it may be the dog that I have been looking for, for two years".

"Could you come today at 4.30pm?"

"Yes... Could I take him home with me when I come along? I also want to stress that I will take the dog, even if it is not the one I have been looking for."

"Oh, I don't think you can take him there and then. We need to let the seven days run its course in case he is claimed. He won't be claimed because the owner did not want him, but just in case."

I was given directions to the pound kennels. It turned out to be about twenty minutes away. I left early and faced a hideous traffic jam. I was being thwarted at every turn! After much stopping and starting, I ultimately made it!

"Could you go and get him?" said the receptionist to one lady.

"I've finished for the day now", she said. Where had I heard that before?! That was reminiscent of two years ago when that had been the sentiment of the dog warden who, despite the reports of the dog being beaten, kicked and starved, had insisted on putting Will back in the house as "what do you expect me to do about it on a Friday afternoon"?

This attitude is so galling. I had worked for two years to get him back. I was stopping him from being put to sleep and had finished my working day too, but I wasn't moaning. So many people go out of their way to help humans or animals in distress, but those who have the power to see positive outcomes through, so often want to clock off on time regardless of the consequences. And they wonder why many of us bond so much with animals!? They are far easier to communicate with!

The receptionist made a call to the kennels and it was arranged for another handler to fetch him. I could not stop telling the people behind the counter about his story as I waited for them to bring him out to me. I was not allowed into the complex, so strained my eyes down the path and watched the CCTV screen in the corner of the room for the first sign of his approach. I felt like I knew this would be him, but I could not think that as what if it wasn't! It was a surreal ten minutes as I went from excited enthusiasm, to relief that I had found him, to despondency that it would not be him.

I went through the story: finding him two years ago, the awful house and threatening dog warden, the people in the street who told us that he was 'kicked, beaten and starved', the liaisons with the organisations I had hoped may help him and the information we had gained that the family had been hurting another dog they had acquired too.

"He's a lovely dog", said the lady behind the counter. "But i'm not sure if he might be a lurcher, not a greyhound".

I showed her the pictures I had taken of him two years ago.

"Could be", she said.

We were all looking at the monitor in the corner of the room now, waiting for him to be brought out on the lead. When he appeared on the screen, I saw a dog straining at the lead, head tilted to the right and legs flailing at the front as he pulled. I knew immediately. It was him!! I could not believe it. I abandoned the screen and shot out of the door behind me. As I went out to meet him, he saw me and pulled more, coming forward as if he knew and remembered me with a quick waggle of the tail. I knelt down on the floor and he nuzzled into me. I cuddled him for a while and told the handler a bit of his story as I said, "Will"..."Matty"... "paw...sit". It was him, but I just had to have him confirm it! The handler must have thought I was totally mad, using two different names and desperately asking this strong dog to sit and give

83

paw!   The handler did not seem remotely interested as he'd only met the dog for the first time that day.

"He seemed to know you" he said dismissively, clearly wanting to get back inside. By this time, Will was looking back at the kennels. I imagine he did not want to get too close to me in case I put him back in that house again. He had remembered though, after two years and all that he had been through.

"I'll see you soon," I promised him. "And this time, I'm not letting you go anywhere".

I could not take him away with me due to the protocol that demanded that the seven days be clear. Doubts had now filled my mind. Was it him? Of course it was! Why was my mind playing tricks on me? I had to wait for the week to be up, but arranged to pick him up at 1pm on Wednesday where he would be signed over to me, all procedures followed.

My beautiful Storm would have to accept him this time, but we would cross that bridge when we came to it. I was over the moon with relief that he was found. It was unimaginable that he had made his way back to us, particularly with so many stray dogs that end up in pounds (and who are put to sleep) across the UK every year. Mum wasn't happy, however, as it meant three dogs! I was not worried about Fleck as she was fine with everyone and everything. The cats would be shocked initially, but they would be ok in time too, as they had when they had met Storm and Fleck. We had four days to gear ourselves up for it. How would I manage four days of further waiting?! But I'd waited two years, so what was four days?!

Chapter Eight:

"He belongs to you now"

The Wednesday morning dawned. I was at the kennels in the morning and 1pm, when I had arranged to pick Will up, seemed like a long way off! I took Storm and Fleck to the kennels with me, bought a lead and muzzle and when 12.30pm came, drove, without the dogs, to the pound. As I pulled into the car park, it felt like this was all happening to someone else. It was the end of my long struggle to find Will, but the beginning of a potential struggle to integrate him into our home. But this didn't matter now. I just had to get him in my hands and out of the pound.

I had to wait for the dog warden to arrive. Every second seemed like a millennium!

"Here he is", said the receptionist as the grey van pulled into the car park.

"Let's do the paperwork before I go and get him", he said.

I signed the papers and he was mine! Officially mine!

"He belongs to you now" said the dog warden. "I would get him microchipped as soon as you can".

"Don't worry", I said, "I intend to do that this evening and will make an appointment as soon as I get home"!

I wanted to ask about the other dogs in the pound. "Do you have many at the moment?"

"Quite a few, a few pedigree dogs too... will you still call him Matty?"

My blood went cold. So this was it. I totally knew that he was Will, but any doubts or worries or little niggles flew away with this statement. Nobody could even question it now.

"...that was the name the homeless man was using for him" the warden was saying.

"That confirms it is the dog I was looking for. They called him Matty but we called him Will", I said. "So I think we'll stick with Will".

"They?" questioned the warden.

"The family who originally owned him".

"He has an owner?"

Not this again, surely.

"No, the family were evicted and nobody knows where they are".

"Oh ok". The warden was chatting to the receptionist now.

I put Will on the lead and proudly took him to the car. I had him! I actually had Will back! It was a bit of a struggle getting him into the car. Perhaps he wondered where he was being taken next. I was careful not to touch his tummy as this was when he had previously got defensive; no doubt further evidence that he had been kicked.

I took him back to the kennels with excitement and relief bubbling up inside me. I introduced the three dogs in the paddocks. I was so euphoric that we had him back, but now reality had to set in. Storm was growling again. Whenever Will came over, Storm would rumble under his breath. I consoled myself that it was not quite as hostile as it had been two years before. The next step was to take them into another neutral environment. I took them into the kennel bungalow to briefly see how they would react in a home environment and off territory. They were fine together! This looked more promising!

I took Will home first as I could not get the three of them in my car. Funnily enough, it was the same car in which we had returned him to the home two years previously. I had not ever dreamt that he would be back in that car and belong to me. Mum came to greet him at the door and I went back to the kennels to collect Storm and Fleck.

Will looked ok. The homeless man must have cared for him. He had more weight than the last time we had known him. He was the same in the way that he sat, gave paw and was fine with the cats. He clearly knew me and of course, Storm did not like him! I still could not get over the fact that he knew me. In the grand scheme of things, we had not had him that long and it had been two years ago!

We would work on the 'Storm' issue! Fleck was absolutely fine and quite pleased to have a new friend to play with in the garden. She bounced around Will, rather intimidating him so that he would run to me for refuge! He was frightened of a little dog in the forest and not aggressive. Those fears were quickly being eliminated. He also kept coming over to give me his paw. Unfortunately, he was suffering from separation anxiety (but who could blame him after all he had been through!). As soon as we moved from our seats, he was whimpering and getting up. Mum was not happy, but all this could be worked on too. Hopefully she would come round as I could not lose him now. At least I had found him and he was safe.

For the first few nights, I slept downstairs on the sofa. Will was in the kitchen and separated from Storm (and Fleck, and me) by a baby gate. Unfortunately, he was so desperate to be with me that he cried and whimpered all night. More difficult was that he was not clean overnight. In order to get to me, he jumped the baby-gate and ran through to the lounge where I was sleeping on the sofa, passing Storm and Fleck. They were both so good that it was like having a whirlwind in the house with the arrival of Will!

We had only had Will for one day when mum went shopping. This would usually be a very uneventful weekly occurrence, but not with Will around and settling in! Mum was still not driving after her hip replacement. We could not risk leaving Will with Storm and Fleck as there was still tension between the boys. We also had a burglar alarm which is linked to the phone. If it goes off, it is the sort of hi-tech system where the police are called. However, if the alarm is not set and we are burgled, we risk being subject to an £80 fine. Not only this, if the alarm goes off, but it is a false alarm, we can also face a call-out charge.

Therefore, with all this in mind, we decided mum would walk to the supermarket, which would be good for her exercise regime, and I would drive to pick her up at the end of the shop.

Now I faced another dilemma. Should I risk leaving the alarm off or should I put Will in a room which did not have an alarm sensor? I chose the latter option – after all, what harm could he do to himself or the house in such a little amount of time? Even if he barked the place down and caused the neighbours grief, it was only going to be for fifteen minutes while I drove down the road, loaded the car with shopping bags and came home again.

Just to be sure that I did not take any chances, I put Will in mum's en suite bathroom and closed the door. He wasn't happy about it but I promised I would not be long and tried to block out the squeaks of protest from my ears. I closed the door to the bedroom too so he was now shut behind two doors before he could come into the proximity of any alarm. Satisfied, I had found a fool-proof method, I went to get mum. As I came up the road, I was pretty confident that Will would still be in the en suite on our return. Inevitably, however, I opened the front door to find Will had come to meet us, wagging his tail in excitement on the other side. The alarm was going off.

"You didn't lock him in anywhere did you?"

"Yes, I closed him behind two doors!" I protested.

"Where?"

"It's ok, I'll look"

"It's not OK, it's absolutely not OK".... mum was starting to go apoplectic again.

Somehow, Will had managed to manoeuvre his way out of two doors, both of which open inwards by pulling the handle down and pulling the door backwards towards himself. This means he would have had to perform this awkward feat with some dexterity... twice! To cap it all, in the process, and presumably in his distress and desperation to find us, he had urinated up mum's bed (in two places), and up her curtains.

Needless to say, mum was furious and I was pretty frustrated too, especially as a row ensued and I had done my best. How was I to know Will was Houdini in disguise? My hope that Will was housetrained had also evaporated and I realised we would have to deal with this as well – something we had never encountered with our other two greyhounds, who had been spotlessly clean.

After about five minutes of shouting, the doorbell rang. I glanced out of the window to see a squad car with flashing lights and another one pulling up behind it.

"Afternoon, has your alarm gone off? What a lovely dog?"...

"Do you want him?" mum joked (or perhaps she was serious).

"He's got a home, mum, thank you"... I said tersely.

"I've got a dog thanks..." refused the police man. "Has your alarm gone off?"

We explained what had happened, and thankfully they were very understanding. We did not ever receive a bill for the call out. Perhaps they recognised that we were totally distraught! Or perhaps they just wanted to make their escape before they ended up going off with a dog in tow!

The police's visit had helped to break up the row at least. What could we do? With no solution in sight, we took the dogs for a walk! Mum and Will were not going to be the best of friends that day, but somehow he always managed to create a redeeming situation.

It was raining so I had to get their waterproof raincoats out of hibernation. Storm was in red, Fleck was in green and Will in bright blue. Will was wearing a cast-off that we had been given from someone for whose dog it was too small. It was a bit big for Will and hung round him, exposing most of his neck and not really serving its purpose. Still, it was better than nothing so it would have to do until we invested in an alternative mac. This bizarre fashion parade in the latest in dog accessories started off down the road. As we turned a corner to head for home, the rain had eased and two children were playing in their garden and spotted us.

"Oooo... look at the doggies" they cried in unison.

We got ready to thrust Fleck forward. We did not want to risk Will yet in children confrontations although he might well be fine to be stroked as he had lived with children. Storm, however, remained very nervous of children due to his traumatic history. Fleck, nevertheless, was a typical greyhound and loved children, letting them pull her around while she stood there gently and patiently. She was happy to be practically sat on or stroked and was wonderful at all the 'meet and greet' events held to tell people about the joys of rescuing a greyhound. Children seemed to gravitate towards her due to her air of total gentleness and her affectionate personality. She would often have us in fits of laughter as she sped around the forest, showing off in front of the other dogs and wiggling her hips as she walked along. Every dog loved her too and when she had had enough, she would sit in a puddle, waiting patiently if we were having a conversation with one of the other dog walkers we met on our route.

Sometimes, unfortunately, children would take Storm as a personal challenge, coming at him, determined that they would succeed in stroking him. Some would succeed, usually when Storm had backed himself into a corner and was cowering on the floor against a brick wall. It can be quite infuriating as Fleck was so amenable to the attention of children, but some parents do not acknowledge that their child should be called away and be satisfied with stroking Fleck.

On this occasion, though, the admiring children were being ushered into a car. Will was, however, the object of their affection: "I like the blue one" stated one child categorically. Will wiggled his tail in affirmation, before dragging me to the nearest grass where he could mark the territory as his own.

With Storm's dislike of Will not abating and Will charging up the stairs at every opportunity with the potential of more urine soaked bedding every time, we tried to think of another method of containing him. Will had an amazing athleticism on the stairs. Usually greyhounds have not encountered stairs before and are very hesitant and reticent on them, especially on the way down. Sometimes they will charge up them in initial exuberance, before being faced with a steep descent and suddenly morphing into an animal existing solely on gangly legs going in all directions! But not Will! He went up and down faster than the speed of light. He followed me up there and back again, thundering by and beating me to the bottom! His feet also made more noise than Storm and Fleck, tapping on the floor like a tap-dancer on acid. I found this amusing, but it did not help mum's irritation as his activeness was so uncharacteristic of the lazy greyhounds. Storm and Fleck would look at him from the comfort of their sofa, thinking "calm down, dear" as he dashed to and fro!

Some people at the kennels had a crate which they had suggested I could borrow. I drove over to them and we hoisted it into the car. This would solve everything.

The wretched thing rattled and bounced all the way home. I was stuck in traffic for half an hour and buffeted around by a sudden gale on a particularly blustery stretch of motorway. We put it together and it just about slotted underneath the work surface in the room which the dogs had taken as their own. Instead of a kitchen table adorned with decorative flowers, this room now contained an old sofa, dog beds and finally, a crate. Will took one look at the crate and promptly got in. As we closed the door, he looked at us with doleful eyes from his new prison. It was quite claustrophobic in there, especially for a dog who had been used to the run of his old house and who did not need to be trapped again. I let him out.

The crate remained in place for a few weeks, but it had all turned out to be a wasted journey as we did not ever use it again!

Will was micro-chipped as soon as we could get an appointment at the vet. This is such a good piece of technology. Now, if he went missing again he could be scanned and traced directly to us. As the chip went in, I breathed a sigh of relief. There would be no more pounds and potential lethal injections as an unclaimed stray.

It is now law that every dog is microchipped. This makes reuniting animals easier and is a cheap and quick process. The peace of mind it brings is unquantifiable. If your dog was to end up in a pound, this would lead him/her straight back to you. As the councils do not have to liaise between boroughs, your dog could end up somewhere which you had not considered. If you did not ring, you would not be reunited with your dog and you would have only seven days before the council determined whether to put your dog to sleep or rehome him/her. If your dog slipped its collar and had no other means of identification on them, this might be the only way of establishing their identity. Sometimes, distraught owners ring pounds but their description could match several dogs and the dog fail to be identified. The consequences of this could mean destruction for your dog; all for the sake of an injection and less than £20 to insert their unique chip. The only downside, of course, is that dogs have to be returned to owners who may not be responsible. Previously, if unclaimed, the dog could be rehomed but now owners must be contacted first.

Will's next episode occurred just a few days later. I left Will with mum when I went to the kennels. I had been taking him with me, but this particular day, there was not a spare kennel in which he could sit. It was not a good move although I had not got much choice as there was nowhere for him to go until I was ready to go home.

Halfway through the day, my mobile rang ominously.

"I've got to go to hospital".... said mum's voice on the other end.

"What?" I replied.

"I've got to go to hospital," mum repeated.

"Why?"

"Will has bitten me".

Again, I went cold. No, he couldn't have done. He was such a good boy really.

"What, how, when, where?" I asked in a panic...

It turned out that Will had gone to run upstairs and mum, thinking he would urinate on her bed again, had understandably grabbed him and lost her temper. Will, also understandably, had turned and nipped her. It was not a great thing, but it was also not a disaster as there was a reason for his defensive behaviour that could be explained by his history. Grabbing him was not something we could do. He could not be manhandled roughly as he would think he was about to be hurt and this could give him cause to turn. He has been so abused and needed an alternative method of discipline. He needed approaching by means of love as he would react to this with more understanding.

Thankfully, this incident was an isolated blip, and when I got back home, mum had been to the local hospital, endured several hours of waiting in A&E, but been given antibiotics, a tetanus booster and gone on her way.

Will was quite subdued that night, knowing what he had done and wanting things to be ok again. He repeatedly came over and offered his paws; left then right then left again. He and mum were reconciled and peace reigned once again over the household.

This calm lasted one night as the following morning, he accidentally met our semi-feral cat, Winnie. Will was now interacting positively with our other cats, Humphrey and Molly. Humphrey had put him in his place by giving him a swipe. Molly was more wary, but was happy to walk into the garden and around the house with Will about. Will had even met a stray cat, whom I had nicknamed Morris, in the garden. We had been feeding Morris and he brazenly appeared over the fence one morning. Will charged up to him and instead of fleeing, which would have undoubtedly encouraged Will to chase him more, he stood his ground and hissed and swore at Will. Will retracted and Morris went on his way!

Winnie, however, was another case altogether. She had come into our care after finding her way to my mum's late Aunt. Auntie had looked after her until a microchip scan established she had an owner. She had to be returned, leaving Auntie distraught. We had had to leave Winnie at the vet so the owners could collect her from there at 6pm. Helpfully, the vet informed us that a little cat was in need of a home at the local animal hospital. We went along and were introduced to a little tabby kitten who immediately climbed into mum's handbag. They agreed that Auntie could adopt her, but only after she was spayed. We could collect her the following week.

The next day, at midday, we received a call from Auntie.

"Winnie is here"...

Oh dear... this was the start of senility. She was obviously not compos mentus.

"Have you taken your tablets today, Auntie?"

"No... Yes... you're not listening to me... Winnie is here"

"But she can't be"

"She is"

"But she can't be... what do you mean?"

"Winnie is here, she got back just now"

"She got back?"

"She's sitting on my bed now and I've given her some salmon flavoured cat food"

"Huh? Where was she?"

"She came through the back door five minutes ago"

"But she can't be, she only went home last night"

"I'm telling you, she's here".

We could hear the delight in Auntie's voice. Winnie, being semi-feral, might have bitten and scratched her, but she loved her and clearly, Winnie knew where she was loved and Winnie loved Auntie. Miraculously, she had been picked up by her owners and made it back to Auntie's in less than a day. There was no way she could have been dropped off nearby as the vet did not know Auntie's address and nobody had given it to the owners. We rang the owners who told us they had collected her last night and, instead of keeping her in for a few days, had let her out again immediately. She had lived above a shop on a busy cross-roads and made it back over busy main roads, covering over three miles, in less than a day! The owners were not too bothered and said Auntie could keep her. This made Auntie's day, but we had another dilemma. We were now left with the little kitten at the hospital who had been so adorable and really needed a home! So Winnie's return prompted the arrival of Molly to a new home with us! Winnie then moved in a year later after Auntie had to go into residential care!

Winnie was much faster and not about often, so yet to be introduced to our new canine arrival. In addition, she and Molly have to be separated as Winnie terrorises Molly, stalking and cornering her. Their stories had been so intertwined and yet she absolutely hates her. She has been known to pin Molly down and will not desist until Molly has fled, preferably with Winnie in hot pursuit to ensure she has total victory. Molly is eight years old but still known as 'the kitten' due to her baby-like behaviour. Humphrey will ignore Winnie's antics, but Molly is utterly petrified. Therefore it is one out in the garden and the other one in! Then, changeover!

Winnie was on her way into the house, when Will appeared and saw her. She saw him and ran! This triggered Will to run too and subsequently, (and totally uncharacteristically), Storm and Fleck joined in too! All three dogs chased Winnie into the garden and as she fled across the patio, I joined in the chase! When she jumped onto the wall, I took my chance to grab her! Being semi-feral, she did not take too kindly to this and went absolutely wild, scratching and biting frenziedly. She gripped my hand and pain shot through it! Fleck and Storm were back inside by this stage, not wishing to engage in more effort than is absolutely necessary, especially first thing in the morning, and thankfully, Will had been put off by the aggressiveness of Winnie!

After being patched up, I went to the kennels with Will and he was with me all day. I did not like leaving Storm and Fleck, but taking Will with me got him out of mum's hair for the day. It also meant that Will was awake all day which might serve to tire him out! Upon our return, we took him out with Storm and Fleck in the forest. This would guarantee that he would be absolutely exhausted. That day, we met some cocker-spaniel puppies and Will was quite frightened by them! They were about six times smaller than him and yet Will was quite overwhelmed!

We reached a mini-breakthrough that night as Will and Storm proceeded to lye together on the floor with us all evening. Fleck was there too, but she was so good that she did not really count when it came to any concerns! Storm's growling had been lessening. It had only been a few days so I felt this signified real progress and we would get there in the end. A major hurdle was gradually being overcome. Will was not presenting any problems in this regard as he wanted to be friends with Storm. He would simply walk away if Storm showed any hostility and would then try again to introduce himself once he thought Storm had relaxed. If there was further resistance from Storm, he would take himself off again. At least Will was not up for a fight to establish supremacy!

Despite all the ups and downs over the first few days, Will was a beautiful dog. He is so affectionate and gentle, despite all he has been through. We did not touch his tummy, however, as we had already been aware of this and it was confirmed when the vet had touched him in that spot upon examination. Will had reacted in warning and turned his head, but thankfully we had anticipated this and put a muzzle on him just in case. This must have been what had happened in the holding kennel two years before. As he had not been in kennels, he was not getting on the bed and they must have been lifting him from his tummy. He had understandably become defensive, especially if he had been routinely hurt in his stomach. He had to use his own defence mechanisms to survive the ordeals he had been put through and who could blame him for that.

He is an exceptionally intelligent and bright dog. He learns quickly and knew his name within one week, despite it not being the name he had been called for the majority of his life. It took Storm about six years to master his name, love him!

Everything was going too well. By the following day, my hand had swollen drastically from Winnie's bite. I battled on regardless and we went to the kennels as we always did the food one day a week for the dogs. We drove up there in two cars, in order to transport the dogs and the food! Mum had plucked up the courage to take to the wheel for the first time after her operation and it enabled the dogs to run around in the paddocks. Will was still wetting overnight so the household was still a bit fraught. However, Storm's gradual improvements in tolerating Will were helping improve matters by making life slightly easier. Will had been given a number and his first course of jabs whilst in the pound, but he needed the follow-up injection in order to complete the course. It was sad to see that Will had simply been number 0716 whilst in the pound when he was actually a wonderful individual, with a life of his own, in his own right.

We decided to take a urine sample with us to the vet the following day when Will went for his vaccinations, in case there was a medical explanation for him being unable to hold it in. Fleck had been suffering from a urine infection when she first came home to us and had had a couple of accidents during her first nights with us. A simple course of antibiotics had sorted this problem immediately. Perhaps we could hope for the same for Will!

However, first there was a medical requirement for my hand. The swelling was very red and starting to creep up my arm. So two days after mum had been in A&E thanks to Will, I was now there, thanks to Winnie (via Will!). It was with some embarrassment and amusement that we parked and waited for my name to be called. I was also given a tetanus booster injection and put onto antibiotics! Of course, nothing is ever simple, so with it being Sunday night, we had to trawl around to try and find a Pharmacy which happened to be open. To make matters worse, it was pouring down with rain and cold and dark. I jumped out of the car several times, only to find the shop closed and see mum driving off as the traffic lights turned green. As I made it up the road, getting soaked in the torrential downpour, I couldn't help recalling the words from the musical, Wicked. After doing her best to help, a series of events had left Elphaba coming off worse. 'No good deed goes unpunished' was swiftly becoming my motto! Eventually, we found an open Pharmacy at the end of our road – sod's law!

I had been sleeping downstairs for a week now. Will was still not settled and he and Storm could not be trusted together, despite the separation of a baby-gate as this presented no barrier to Will. The final straw that sent me back to my bedroom was when Will kept me awake, crying all night from midnight until 6.25am. My alarm went off at 6.30am!

I tried to ignore him, but at 3.30am, I had had enough of the squeaking and went out and shouted at him. I felt so guilty afterwards as he reacted to this by cowering on the floor. This poor, lovely dog must have suffered so terribly and here I was, the one he wanted to be with, shouting at him. At 5am I took him around the garden. He was still squeaking, so I concluded I would need to get some rest and the following night, I slept in my bed again. He slept in until 6.45am, but he
98

had wet again, twice. The urine sample had shown that there was no infection present. I knew he would get there with the house-training, but I wished he would hurry up about it!

Chapter Nine:

"NO"!

Sleeping upstairs gave me some much needed rest as Will's squeaking was only exacerbated if he knew I was there. The three dogs were getting on better now – ten days after Will came home. Storm had thankfully, for the most part, stopped growling and, although they got a little rough in the garden, they lay together in the sitting room with us in the evening.

Although Will had proven to be excellent with the cats, (with the exception of the Winnie episode!), the same could certainly not be said when it came to the foxes in the garden at night. We always take the dogs out for a final toilet trip and took Storm and Fleck along the road for a mini-walk. Fleck would not take any notice as the foxes and cubs followed us like the Pied Piper of Hamlin down the road. Winnie would often follow too, making it a totally ludicrous scene! I'm sure the neighbours had a good laugh at this spectacle! Storm would look at the foxes and often lose concentration. Watching them was far more interesting and exciting than going to the toilet. The only problem this presented was having to walk further than might otherwise be necessary in order to remind him to focus on the task in hand!

Will, on the other hand, caught me by surprise. The first time I had taken them out, I had nonchalantly walked out of the front door with him, only to be towed along the road like a scene from Ben Hur. No matter how much I shouted, 'No', and pulled him back, he would bark and yank me forward. There was nothing for it, we would have to go out into the back garden! On the road, the foxes could come from any doorway, any garden and any direction. In our back garden, at least Will would be contained and the foxes would only have our garden in which to appear.

From then on, Fleck would accompany me off the lead in the garden, totally trustworthy with whatever appeared, especially if Winnie was around, while I took Storm and then Will around on the lead.

Sixteen days after he first came home, or rather, after he came home for the second time, Will was clean overnight. When we came downstairs in the morning, Storm and Fleck were always delighted to see us and Storm would put both front feet on the baby-gate in excitement, while Fleck craned her neck, smiling over the top. Will was also getting more and more close to us and, at the time of writing, whenever I go out for the evening, the joy and welcome he displays upon my return is quite moving. Of course, I am equally delighted to see him too and always know my special friend will be waiting for me when I get in. It helps to pass the time if the evening is not living up to expectation! Initially, I was careful not to over-fuss him on returning, but he is so excited that we do have a huge hug once he has calmed down. He puts both his front legs on my shoulders and bounces as we embrace with laughter and lots of tail wagging! His tail wag always amuses me. Storm and Fleck would wag their whole tail, but Will's tail is more curly and appears to waggle at the tip!

Calm is not always something Will understands. Although he sleeps once settled, he is not as lazy as a typical greyhound. Going for walks is often an excuse for skidding up and down, barking, jumping and grabbing my arm. He has obviously been watching too many 'police-chase' programmes on the television, as he has the German Shepherd rugby tackle down to a tee. As much as we try to discourage this, he continues. People have suggested various calming methods, but none of these has yet worked. I think he is so used to noise and threats that nothing we do will stop him. I now find it an endearing part of his character; he is just a loveable nightmare!; but I'm not sure I can say the same for mum, whose blood pressure rises whenever the leads rattle.

We had not had Will back for very long when we picked Tommy up again. It was a day when mum came to the kennels too so we went in two cars. I took Tommy and Fleck while mum had Will in the boot and Storm on the back seat. Fleck was pleased as this was another potential friend to enjoy. Her tail wagged with excitement when she saw him and, with a big grin on her face, she took some convincing to stay on the back seat while Tommy stood in the boot.

When we had first picked Tommy up, he had lost a lot of weight and we had had to urge the owner to up the food. Positively, over the last few months, he had gained weight, but there was a new problem. The owner was quite distressed as she wanted him to come upstairs with her, but he could not manage the very steep stairs in her house. We tried several times to take him up and down, but he froze on the spot and would not attempt the climb, let alone the descent. He was coming into kennels more and more frequently and our suspicions were being raised about whether or not he was actually really wanted. It seemed that the owner wanted a break from him. It transpired that she wanted to bring him to the kennels for four months from September to January. This was madness. The coldest time of the year is the time when these dogs should be in homes, particularly if they are used to homes and out of kennel routine. We asked her to be honest with us and she finally admitted that she was struggling. She loved Tommy very much, but was worrying if he did not eat or if he did not come in from the garden or if he did not go upstairs. She was clearly panicking and instead of getting into a routine, had let the worry override everything. She was taking him to the vet more frequently than we deemed necessary and it was starting to cross our minds that we might be faced with another Gus scenario. After much deliberation, she decided to give him back to the kennels to find a new home.

It was a bizarre case, but I could not help think that if Tommy had not been in that home, we would probably not have got Will back. If I had not been delivering Tommy back home that day, I may not have seen the door of Will's old house open or discovered that the family had moved out. I will always be thankful to Tommy.

102

Tommy was back at the kennels for a few months before he really landed on his feet. A lovely couple journeyed for an hour to choose a dog and Tommy has become their pride and joy. He has not had any problems and has an absolutely wonderful life where he is completely doted upon. He climbs the stairs now and his diet is sorted too. He is another of the dogs who was really lucky in the end.

We were socialising Will a little with Mabel and Stanley, the two dogs we walked for our friend. Presumably, Will had not been walked in his previous home so other dogs were a novelty to him. This would also explain the overwhelming excitement when it came to 'going walking'! He had picked up this phrase almost immediately, and would stir from a deep sleep to frantic rushing back and forth, tail wagging at the prospect. Although we knew that he had lived with a Staffie in the past, he was always very excited when he saw another dog. Walking with Mabel and Stanley helped to integrate him a little with other breeds. Tragically, their owner had now died and her adult children worked during the day so we continued to take the dogs out for them. We used the muzzle on Will initially, but after a few walks, he was no trouble at all with them. There was no aggression in him, just occasional 'bull in a china shop' rushing where he was not too sure about canine etiquette in certain situations. Fleck would also help as she was so good with every other dog we met that Will could follow her example. He was also copying Storm who used his hind legs to kick back at the ground after going to the toilet, redesigning the forest as he went. Will would follow suit, and Fleck, who often followed behind, would emerge with mud and leaves covering her head or back!

It was lucky that the muzzle was not necessary because Will had quickly learned to take it off! He would rub and push it off his head. We tried to fool him by putting a different type of muzzle on him, but he removed this at an even faster pace by using his dew claw as a thumb and hooking it off his head! Our next trial was a material muzzle but he shook this off after two minutes, meaning we then had to hunt around for it for about half an hour!

On the lead, Will would bark at other dogs whenever he saw them and pull and strain to get near them. Owners of some other breeds would back off in horror as Will nearly garrotted himself to try and get to their dog. One owner, however, whose dog was a beautiful rescued black spaniel called, 'Sam', was more obliging and said Will could go up to Sam if he wished. Will dragged me over and when he had sniffed Sam, he wagged his tail and went down on his front legs like he wanted to play. He clearly was not going to be a problem with other dogs and was so intelligent that coming off the lead in due course was bound to be a reality. Mabel was the same with other dogs. If she was on the lead she would be an absolute nightmare, barking and pulling; but once set-free, she would happily interact with any dog she came across.

Barking was not something we had experienced with Storm and Fleck. Fleck never barked at home, although at the kennels she would play in the paddocks and bizarrely bark at the other dogs! Storm was the same, although after four years with us he had started to 'woof' twice if the doorbell rang. Fleck would run to the door, with Storm following at a distance. This was an improvement as he had previously fled to the furthest point of the house at the slightest hint of a visitor.

Will, however, barks at every given opportunity! He barks at unexpected and unforeseeable noises or events. Sometimes, he can be inconsistent too, meaning we gear ourselves up for lunatic barking which then does not materialise! He initially barked at thunder and then at the noise on the television programme, QI when the buzzers go off! He also leaps up barking at the BBC logo which breaks up programmes. However, he does not make a sound for the logo which features dogs running in a circle, but only the logo featuring a forest scene! He also got very irate with the bell that goes off prior to a trial on I'm A Celebrity Get Me Out of Here, something I had not even heard until Will took a great dislike to it. He barks at the doorbell, he howls at the telephone and he barks at the footsteps of the postman coming up the path, trying to grab the mail as it comes through the letterbox! I wish I knew if these things reminded him of something untoward in his history. Although this is another reason for mum to be heard cursing his antics, many people do comment that barking at the door-bell is actually quite a good thing!

Barking before walks is the main reason for us yelling 'no'! The skidding, mouthing and barking continues no matter what we do. Despite all our efforts, in his zealous enthusiasm, he still thinks he is a police-dog, grabbing criminals.

When playing in the garden, he does chase a ball and enjoys a variety of toys, particularly Fleck's string of fake sausages, which he grabs, shakes and with which he then charges around waving frantically, before dropping them, rushing about madly and then lunging at my arm! Nevertheless, he is totally devoted to me. When I am in the garden, he jumps on the sofa, front legs on the back, watching me through the window. This was another cause of 'No, Get down' echoing round the house as mum bellowed her irritation at Will's chaotic behaviour. Will, realising this was viewed as naughty, decided to get up against the back cushions and rest his head on the back so he could continue to peer out of the window! The pitiful look on his face really pulls at the heart-strings too. In addition, Will would still come over at home and give his paws compulsively, one paw and then the next from a sitting position, looking at you with big doleful eyes. He certainly knows how to make your heart melt and this often results in a big hug (from me) and pulled faces (from mum)!

Fireworks, however, were things that did not cause Will any fear! This could not be said for Fleck, who would shake, salivate and hide behind the sofa. Storm would pull back to the house, tail between his legs and ears back if an unexpected 'bang' was let off during a walk. Will, however, was totally un-phased. I could walk him around the block without any worry of him having any adverse reaction. No matter how loud, he would still behave as if nothing was going on. I expect this does reflect his history and the noises and pandemonium of his previous household which he must have endured.

I have nothing against fireworks per se, but I do feel that they should, at the very least, be limited. There should be some regulation which necessitates that the noise should not exceed a certain level of decibels as sometimes the sound of the explosions is like bombs repeatedly blasting into the night. In addition, there should be a cut-off time so they cannot be let off after, for example, an 11pm watershed; nor set off before 5.30pm. Moreover, it should be declared that it is acceptable for one day only out of the calendar per year. Currently, fireworks start in October and continue for weeks! This leads to weeks of frustrating nights when petrified pets undergo unnecessary fear. I dread to think what it must induce in wild animals. Not only that, of course, letting off loud explosions late into the night on week nights, is not fair on workers or children.

We continued to take the dogs up to the kennels with us on a Sunday. I would take Will with me during the week, but seeing all three dogs in the paddock together was lovely. Fleck was always a star and Will and Storm were fine together now. We had noticed, however, that Fleck was not as keen to go on walks as she had been. Normally she would stretch (do her exercises) and get up, tail wagging, head on one side with a grin on her face and come padding to the front door. She seemed to be slowing down and I was very worried as there appeared to be a swelling on her leg. I feared the worst, thinking it was the dreaded cancer, and so we made an appointment for a scan at the vet. With trepidation, we took her in for the day and waited anxiously by the phone. When the phone rang, I did not want to hear the results, but thankfully, our worst fears were proven incorrect and she was given the all clear. It turned out to be a chipped bone in her leg for which she was given painkillers and sent home. What a huge relief for our special girl who was just as delighted to be home as we were to have her back.

At the kennels, several months before, we had taken in a beautiful lurcher who was named, 'Benji'. He was adorable as he had shaggy fur and was ever so friendly, giving cuddles whenever he could and generally looking scruffy and appealing. He had come in from the pound and was emaciated, covered in fleas and needing a good bath on his arrival. He was adopted by a lovely couple who renamed him Fred (as they already had a beautiful black greyhound called Barney and wanted to continue the Flintstones theme!).

One week, we were joined at the kennels by the couple, Jeff and Kim, who had adopted Barney and Fred, formerly Benji. Jeff, who has had a long-term passion and interest in lurchers, took one look at Will and said, "He's a lovely lurcher."

"Lurcher?"

The thought had crossed our minds as he was far more energetic than the greyhounds, which could indicate a cross with another breed, making him a lurcher, a cross between a sight-hound and another breed. Lurchers are very similar to greyhounds in their temperament and demeanour. We had wondered whether Will was a cross with 'something else', but the young boy in his original home had told us he was a greyhound.

"He's definitely a lurcher, he's fantastic. If he wasn't your dog, I would definitely want him", said Jeff. "I think he's crossed with a Collie".

Well, this would explain why he was energetic and perhaps behaved similarly to Mabel, a Border Collie, when he was on the lead.

Will was still pulling on the lead like a steam-train. We were due to attend a greyhound gathering with the kennels and would be taking Storm, Will and Fleck. I still found it amusing that mum, who had needed heavy convincing to allow me to adopt one dog, now had three!

In the week leading up to the gathering, I carried out my usual tasks at the kennels. Fleck's leg was still causing her trouble so she was not going on long walks any more. We had to realise she was getting older, but hopefully rest and gentle exercise would mean she could resume her usual charging around, off-lead ways in the forest (and mud) before too long.

I would take Will with me to the kennels and on a Monday, mum would join me there, bringing Storm and Fleck along for the afternoon. I loved seeing them coming through the gate, wagging their tails and smiling as they came over to me; their expectant faces full of loving joy as well as smiles and fun. They were devoted to each other and Fleck had been wonderful for Storm, bringing him out of his shell and helping him so much to regain his confidence after his fearful start in life.

On the day of the gathering, we convened at the kennels and travelled in two cars to the meeting area. We had bought Will a 'non-pull' harness/lead. It really worked! We walked with all the other greyhounds and I had no problems at all! This lead was amazing!! I took Will and Storm on the long walk and mum stayed with Fleck, who had made herself comfortable on a duvet near the raffle prizes! She could not cope with the whole walk, but if mum stayed with her, she would be ok. I wasn't happy for mum to do the whole walk either, with her new hip. I later, learned, however, that both of them had made it to the lake and back, but had not walked all the way around it. It's a shame, as in normal circumstances, Fleck would have loved being with the other dogs, wallowing in the lake and meeting passers-by. She was so well behaved and we could trust her with anything, babies prodding and poking her and any dog she met whilst out and about.

The lead worked really well for Will. He was no trouble throughout the whole afternoon and it was a lovely event as we were visited by a few familiar faces. Dandy had come with his owners to see us and been joined by one of their other dogs, Charley V (renamed Zak), who sadly had had to have a leg amputated. Will lay down at my feet and behaved impeccably. It was only when we got home that we removed the harness and found it had rubbed at his fur and legs. He had sore red marks under his arm-pits and the poor love must have been experiencing discomfort for most of the walk. However, he had still been a very good boy, and it was nice to know he could walk successfully around other dogs, albeit that these had mainly only been other greyhounds.

Interestingly, one of the volunteers who came along to the event, has a dog who is so very similar to Will, that in the past, before we got Will back, seeing 'Eddie' used to tear at the heartstrings as he so reminded me of Will in colour and size. I had had to do a double-take the first time I had seen him, as I had also done on a different occasion when I had seen a dog similar to Will walking down the lane from the other kennel. It turned out that a friend of Les, Eddie's owner, lives in the area where Will used to reside. He relayed a story to me about an incident his friend had once told him:

"One day, he was walking down the road with his own dog, not a greyhound, when he spied a dog following them. The dog was off the lead and seemed lost and unaccompanied. He could not get hold of this stray dog because of his own dog, but as they turned back, they saw it was a greyhound that was following them. They phoned me to see if Eddie was ok and had not got loose. Apparently he was the spitting image of Eddie".

As Les retold this story, I was reminded of another lady who had adopted one of our kennel dogs and had seen Will wandering on his own on one occasion. How many times had he been out loose? It makes you wonder. Surely, he was not just let out to roam. But then the chances of me being where he was at the same time, would have been astronomically low. If he had been picked up on other occasions, he was presumably returned to the irresponsible home. The law in this regard should be amended so that ownership is not enough if a dog is clearly not looked after. It made me appreciate even more how important it was that I could not have walked away and left him. Who else would have helped him? People either did not care, felt it was not their job (which is tantamount to the same thing) or did not know so would not have been doing anything about it anyway. Poor Will had had no one to defend him, no one who was prepared to help him and nobody to turn to if he was being beaten, kicked or starved.

Hearing Les' testimony was strange – to know someone, albeit indirectly connected to me, had seen Will, alive, at the time I had been most worried about him was a funny feeling. If I had known at the time, it might have given me hope, but at the same time, caused even more frustration as it would have been unconfirmed whether or not it had been Will at all.

Funnily enough, I experienced the same feeling when, after being reunited with Will, it came to light that a friend of mum's, who lived not too far from Will's road, had a neighbour who had been a friend of Will's family and had been in the house. Apparently, he had seen Will and been afraid of him. Will had presumably had to defend himself by warding off any threats. He was certainly not an aggressive dog. Sometimes, he did exhibit behaviour that would be reminiscent of his past. He had initially growled at a friend when they visited and been anxious if people tried to fuss him whilst he was on his bed. But we respected these anxieties and left him, telling people not to touch him if he was on the bed or sofa. However, this was certainly not a huge problem and, as time went on, it became increasingly less obvious. If he does wake from a deep sleep with a growl, he realises where he is and immediately gets off the sofa to come and give his paw in apology.

Now, when coming in from the garden, Will often makes a rush for the sofa in order to get there first and bag the best seat! He will then sit up grandly, proud of himself while Storm stands and looks despondently, once again realising he has been too slow to gain the comfortable sofa and been relegated to the bed on the floor. However, when we ask Will to get off the sofa and move over, he resignedly comes off, climbing back on simultaneously with Storm in order to share the seat together. They have come a long way from the days where Will could not even walk past him in the hall.

One thing that was really starting to grate on my nerves was people calling Will, 'Wills'. I appreciate that this was not going to cause mass murder or huge waves of starvation, but I really find it annoying!

"His name is, Will" I wanted to shout, while wringing their necks.

"How is Wills... is little Wills ok...?"

Of course, mainly people were only being kind when asking after his welfare, but I could not understand why an 's' was put on the end of his name. I was tempted to do the same back to them: "Yes, he's fine, thank you, Pauls, Peters, Johns, Fredas, how are you?"

Others really sent my blood boiling: "So you still have Wills?"...

"Yes, of course, and you still have your repulsive children?"...

(Clearly I left out the 'r' word in this latter sentence, however tempted I was to include it!)

Chapter Ten:

"More the Knowledge, Lesser the Ego, Lesser the Knowledge, More the Ego" (Albert Einstein)

As I have said in previous pages, the Kennels is an amazing place for extremes in human behaviour. At one end of the spectrum are those who are so totally genuine. They go with one thing in mind (and one thing only), namely the welfare of the dogs. Their sincerity can be quite moving at times when they dedicate time (and often money) to the cause without seeking any (or excessive) praise or affirmation. Sometimes, of course, we all need a boost, but those I have in mind who cause trouble are individuals for whom ego plays the only or biggest part. Often these people shout the loudest in an arrogant way about the very minor part they play, praising no one else and expecting unwarranted glorification for the most insignificant of things. When this recognition and perceived praise is not heaped upon them, they become petty and small minded. Often this immature behaviour is accompanied by jealousy which only serves to highlight their laughable position. Thankfully the latter set of people often leave when they can't get what they want. It seems this affliction is a scourge to many organisations, but it never fails to leave me baffled. I suppose it comes down to the fact that those who know they do their best do not need to prove this to others, but most of all to themselves. Therefore, those who do a lot stay quiet or just confide in those closest to them, whilst others have to justify their existence to everyone. Funnily enough, however, if the latter bunch stayed quiet or laughed about it, they would receive more respect!

Of course, there are also those who come looking for dogs who we have to turn away. Sometimes these are blatantly lying, underhandedly hostile and unkind or, in the case of one family, frightened of the dogs. The latter family was a very strange visit as the wife was clearly under the control of her husband and, I would not be surprised if she was the victim of domestic abuse at his hands. There was no way I was going to let a dog go there! Then you compare this with such kind people who offer homes where you know the dogs will be going to a wonderful life where they will be loved as they deserve. One lucky dog, Boris, went with a lovely couple who were both medical consultants. Another two have gone to a fireman and his exceptionally caring wife; others have gone to people from all walks of life and all professions. The dogs do not have much in their lives and the least they long for is a comfortable bed, decent food and the chance of a caring home life. Of course, a loving home is the main criterion for saying 'yes' to a home. It does not matter if you live in a one roomed flat or a mansion if you are 'nice' and prepared to love the dog.

It is always lovely when you get people visiting who we can tell will give the dog a lovely home. It helps if they have a couple of brain cells to rub together and can absorb what we are saying. Sometimes, you do wonder how people get through life. I was speaking to one chap from the kennel next door who was an ex-marine, having worked in Afghanistan. I happened to join him on the field one day when he was walking a spaniel.

"Do you get 'them' as well?"

"Them?" I responded.

"You know", he said, with a roll of the eyes... "them"...

"oh *them*"I said knowingly. "Yes, I'm afraid we do"

"We had one couple in the other week who were asking if we could help them with their dog. They had absolutely no ability to handle him whatsoever. The dog was not listening to a word they said. I tried to work with him for a while, but it was clear that the main problem was a lack of socialisation. I said to them, I'm going to go and get a placid dog – I think that will help".

"Right" I interjected. "And what did they say?"

"They said, (and at this moment, this ex-marine put on a high-pitched, estuary English accent), "he's gonna go and get a plastic dog 'e said.

Yeah that's right, nah, you can't have no chewing gum. It ain't time for your dinner yet".

How do these people survive?!

Once a month, Mum takes an elderly lady home after her lunch at the local centre. The centre happens to be on the same road as Will's previous address.   We would go to the kennels and, on the way home, collect the lady and I would sit, or rather, be squashed in the back of the car with the dogs while we delivered her to her address. When we only had Storm, I would take him into the hall with me, whilst we waited for the lunch to end. However, with the proximity of Will's previous abode being too close for comfort, I determined to stay in the car with the dogs rather than risk parading him on the streets for ex-neighbours or potentially passing friends of the old family to see him. Mum would go in and fetch the old lady, hopefully not removing her from her dinner sooner than she expected!

On one particular occasion, the only parking space available was so dangerously close to his former home that I was on edge for the whole wait! Hours and hours seemed to pass. The dogs were getting restless and I was scanning the windows for any signs of people who might do a double-take or pause, point and scream. I sat there frozen to the spot, not daring to draw any attention to the car when a couple of people went by who seemed to go into a house nearby. My heart was in my mouth. The tension in the car was at its highest when the windows started to steam up. This might provide us with some cover!

Where was mother!? Why on earth had it taken so long? Eventually, I saw her slowly making her way to the car with her charge in tow. I was not going to go through that again! From now on, we would go home with the dogs before picking up the elderly lady!

In the two weeks after the walk and kennel gathering, Fleck was still slowing down. She joined me on the evening walks less and less and, although I didn't like leaving her at home, the two boys got a faster walk and Fleck could potter in the garden at her own pace.

Will was still accompanying me to the kennels and he behaved reasonably well. Although, when he sees me, he can start squeaking, sometimes even howling! He can be a hooligan and does seem to find and gravitate to the mud in the paddocks and need a good hosing down afterwards. Strangely, he will step over this when out and about on walks. I took him with me one day when the kennels were very full and there was no kennel space.

"I'll have to put him in the hallway of the bungalow and close the door," I said.

"Do you need a hand"?

"No, I'll just move all the stuff and then he can't wreck the joint"

"No"

I went into the bungalow and shifted anything that looked remotely breakable, damageable, smashable, rippable or moveable. I made up a nice duvet with snugly blanket and put a bowl of water in the hallway, closing the doors to the bedrooms and kitchen. There was nothing he could touch. It was totally 'Will-proof'. I collected him from his mud bath, cleaned him and stuck him in the bungalow, closing the door behind him. The door was a stable-door so the base stayed shut and the top part shut separately.

"What was that?" said my colleague.

"What?" I said.

"That click?"

"I didn't hear anything".

When I went back outside, Will was peering out of the door. I could have sworn I had shut that door behind me. I must be going mad. So I gave him a quick head-rub and shut the door.

"I've just shut the door to the bungalow" said my colleague.

"Did I not just shut that"?

"No, it was open – must be the wind"

This was peculiar. Will was squeaking behind the door so I resigned myself to a day of noise.

Click.

"Did you hear that?" I said. "I keep hearing a clicking".

"Someone must be going in the bungalow – I'll get the broom".

"But Will's in there"

Armed with this makeshift weapon, we bravely went round to the door. Will was looking at us, a huge smile on his face, paws on the bottom of the door. When he saw us, his tail started flapping with excitement and he bounced up and down with enthusiasm.

"Has someone come past you?" I asked Will. His tail wagged even more at the possibility of an escape from his confine coming his way.

"Are you sure?" I questioned him more.

"There's no sign of anyone in here" said my colleague after a while.

We closed the door again and 'click'. There was Will, looking over the doorframe again.

"It's Will"!!!!!!!!! "He's opening the door", we both exclaimed.

Of course, Will can open doors! How stupid of me to forget this after the burglar alarm incident. He was pushing down on the handle and pulling the top of the door towards him. This was the clicking sound! You can't take him anywhere!

Whether he was in the bungalow or the kennel, he would spend his time up at the door, gazing out pitifully. When it is time to go home, he becomes uncontrollable. He is poised like an athlete ready to take off from the start line; body leaned back ready to give himself full blast off power. He barges from the kennel, tail waving frantically and half dragging me down the passage to the gate! Weirdly, the other dogs seem to sense that he is different as they all leap up at their doors to see who the incumbent is! This causes Will to bark in defence and chaos reigns in a formerly peaceful kennel as we try, with no avail, to leave as calmly as possible!

The day often concludes with Will causing mayhem to himself too! He is very accident prone. One day he would cut his leg in the paddock; another time he would graze his paws. Once, there had been no empty kennels again for him to wait in so he had had to go in the treatment room. Late in the morning, an almighty crash emanated from Will's vicinity (who else!?). When I got him out, a trail of blood followed him down the corridor. Why was it always Will!? The treatment table had fallen on him now and I had to wrap his leg up so he sported another colourful bandage.

One Sunday night, I gave some chicken to each dog before their bedtime. Fleck went to take hers, but missed and one of the other two got it. We didn't think anything of it, but the next day, when we woke up, she was lying on her side and she did not respond. We have always rushed animals to the vet, sometimes unnecessarily and too quickly, so when I sat with her and helped her up, we thought we were panicking too soon as she went into the garden and walked around. We left her at home that afternoon while we went to the kennels, something we will always regret. When we arrived home, she was standing behind the sofa, against the radiator, under the window. We coaxed her out and she drank some water.

I wish I had slept downstairs with her that night, but we went to bed as normal. The next morning, Tuesday 19th July 2010, Fleck was on the floor, had vomited and been unable to move from it. She could lift her head, but did not get up of her own volition. I managed to scoop her up and stand her up so that we could clean up the mess, but she was barely moving and needed immediate veterinary attention. We phoned the vet and were able to take her as soon as we could get there. I carried her to the car and I did not realise this would be the last time Storm would see his friend. She was carried into the vet and then proceeded to walk around the room, albeit at an angle which suggested a possible stroke. We thought she could come home while we waited for blood test results, but it was then felt best if she stayed at the vet so that she could be put onto a drip to ensure proper hydration. We could do nothing, but go home and wait.

Time ticked by, interspersed by feelings of panic and hope interchangeably. Surely this could not be the end for our beautiful and perfect little Fleck. Storm would be utterly desolate without his special friend. She had so much more to enjoy. It would be her birthday in August when she would be eleven years old. She was only ten years old. For some reason I took to doing a puzzle which featured two cheetahs. It was an impossible mission as there were 1000 pieces and every single one seemed to be the same colour!

Suddenly my mobile rang. I leapt upon it and then hesitated, fearing to hear the news I was dreading. The news was not good. The blood results were all over the place. We had the option of putting her to sleep there and then or doing one further test to rule out other possibilities. We opted for the latter – we had to give her a chance. The waiting continued but with a terrible cloud casting a shadow of despair across the day.

It was decided to take her to the hospital, about ten minutes away. We went back to the vet and the sight of her on the table will remain with me forever. As she saw us come in, she lifted her head and, despite her weak state, her little flecky tail with the brown patch where the fur was thinner, went thump, thump as it wagged on the table. We had to be with her, to reassure her and to be together. She came in my car as we followed the vet to the hospital, the same hospital as we had first seen Will just over two years before. There we had no choice but to leave her in their care, stressing that we were to be contacted in the event of any change or if any decision had to be taken. We wanted to be with her. We went home and the waiting agony continued.

When the call came, it was utterly mind-numbing. They had performed an ultrasound and found a tumor attached to her heart that had ruptured and was shutting down all her organs. There was nothing to be done but to go to her and take the kindest decision to free her from this world and her pain. We travelled to the vet in a daze – could this really be true? Was this really happening? Our special little girl, so full of love and enjoyment, who had been through so much and found her home with us; and who had given Storm so much confidence; was not going to walk back home that night.

She was in a cage and lifted her head when she saw us. I got on the floor with her and squeezed her, holding her tightly to me as much as I could. She had a drip in her front leg and we could see the bare patch on her side where the ultrasound had taken place. Her little grey face looked up at me as they loaded the needle which would take her pain away but bring us such heartache. As she fell asleep peacefully, I kissed her repeatedly and she knew she was loved. The agony of her loss is indescribable. The grief of losing her was so immense that it blew your mind and left you utterly devastated and inconsolable. You exist in a dream-like state for several days and weeks, missing them so much and being reminded of their individual character as you walk the area they loved and enjoyed, without them. Everything is bleak in those first days and weeks as you are confronted with a life without them. I continued with my puzzle in remembrance of her and went to the kennels in a robotic, 'going-through-the-motions-but-not-fully-there' like state. Will and Storm were, of course, a wonderful comfort, but the pain of grief is a burden so great that it occupies every waking moment. There is no break from it. When they howled in the morning, there was a little voice missing; when we prepared the food, we only needed two bowls instead of three; when walking, we passed the puddles she wallowed in, but no smiling face would be gazing out of them now. As time wears on, however, these agonising memories turn to joyful memories as you remember with thankfulness that time you shared together and the moments to treasure. Then you feel them watching over you, still with you and accessible in an unbreakable bond. How lucky we were to have known her and have her in our lives. The vision of a joyous reunion as expressed by the 'rainbow bridge' poem is something that can get you through. Reading the poems from others who have lost much loved animal friends is an emotional experience, often leaving tears streaming down your face; but it is also a comfort as death is not the end; as well as connecting you with others sharing your experience.

Losing a loved animal can be a very isolating experience. For some reason, human friends do not understand and many will offer initial comforting noises and expect that to be enough. They don't realise that you are not interested in the petty nonsense of every day life the next time you meet. It takes far more than a one off utterance of consolations to get back on track. You have lost a loved one so close to you; someone you shared every day with and with whom you shared more genuine love than you do with the majority of human beings. Sometimes, of course, at the end of a long life, the pain of loss is no less, but may be easier to take and bear if there is a long life or a release from suffering.

The important thing, too, is never to say you could not adopt again due to the awful pain of loss. There are so many needy animals who need a warm bed and love. Where would Fleck have been if we had thought that way after losing our precious cats: Pudding, Mitzi, Arthur and Freddie; as well as all the other animals we have ever loved. Of course, adopting another will never replace the one lost. Every individual, whatever their species, is unique and irreplaceable. Nobody will ever be Fleck and nor would we want them to be. Moreover, Fleck would never be whoever might come along in the future. Adopting another animal does not have to happen immediately, but when the time is right, another needy soul can find a place in your home and in your heart as well as enrich your life. Bonds with our animal friends are so special that to envisage a life without animals is inconceivable. This connection is expressed by many who have felt moved to take pen to paper after the loss of a loved animal friend. It is a widespread feeling amongst those who know this love and is so well described by the rainbow bridge poem: the animal in heaven gets the call that their loved human is coming and, looking up, they see you, recognition spreading between you and them and you are reunited in ecstatic joy as they run towards you, accompanying each other across the bridge, together forever. Another comforting poem also expresses this. It is spoken from the perspective of the beloved departed animal looking over you, "be patient, live your journey through, then come home to be with me".

Looking at the photographs of Fleck was both therapeutic and painful. One of the last photographs of her was at the kennel gathering. She was sitting next to the table which held the drinks, nestled on a duvet, soaking up the view and sitting with some other dogs. Checking my emails again only days later, it was very sad to see that Charley V had also lost his battle for life. He had also been at the gathering and, despite being on three legs, had done so well to walk across the field. Someone else was now going through the same agony as us.

Chapter Eleven

"Here we are again!"

Sometimes we feel that we need to take up permanent residence in the vet. Storm was clearly missing Fleck, yet we did not want to risk Storm and Will being together at night. So Will was still in the kitchen and Storm in the next room, separated by the restored baby-gate. However, we did not take the same precautions when we took them to the kennels. They were happy in the paddocks together and happy to share a kennel where they could sit until we were ready to go home.

One afternoon, six days after losing Fleck, they were out in the paddocks together for over two hours while we let the other dogs out up at the kennels. It was a beautiful day and the temperature not too hot, meaning they could sit outside and enjoy the fresh air. As I pottered up to the dog in the end kennel, suddenly, there was a terrible screaming. An almighty fight had broken out, perhaps triggered by a loveable, but lively dog who was running about next to them in the adjacent run. Typically, I was as far away as I could be and, as I ran towards them, I could do nothing but watch them tumble over each other as they wrestled together on the ground along the fence. When I reached them, they had separated. Will had a nasty wound on his leg and shoulder and Storm had injured ears and had lost a canine tooth. So less than a week after being at the vet with Fleck, we were back, having to make a visit with both boys. Why was it that everyone else had tranquil, harmonious inter-relationships with their dogs, whilst ours were doing this!?

It was rather odd to be in the same room where Fleck had walked around less than a week before, but the boys had to go back again the following day to be sown back together! So exactly a week to the day after Fleck, we were leaving Storm and Will at the vet to each have an anaesthetic. Leaving them there was another numbing experience as it necessitated worrying about two! Storm was very worried as he is fearful of new situations after all he has been through. He looked to me for reassurance, but I could not stay with him. Will, too, needs that security as the last time he had been on his own in a similar place was when he was in the pound. I hoped they would not be too distressed until it was time for their operation and until we were back to pick them up that evening. Thankfully, both came through fine, albeit with a few more stitches and patches than before!

The funny thing was that Will was changing colour anyway! Presumably from where he had been outside with the homeless man, he had almost been bleached by the sun! His colour was becoming more uniform over his body rather than a line down his back that differed from the rest of him! As I write, he is curled up next to me on the sofa, resting his head on my lap and leaning into me. There is snow on the ground outside and we are snuggled up together – something I had always dreamt of, but never believed would be possible when we were looking for him. It is still amazing that we have him back. Sometimes I look at him and can't believe it; as well as wishing we had not missed out on those two years together and that he had not been through an additional two years of hurt during that time.

To have the boys back home and well was wonderful – what a relief! They are so lovely and they were pleased to be home too! We could hear them when we got in the vet! There was no need to tempt them out or coax them with chicken slices. They were off and away and very quick to leap into the car!

Will was really coming on. He is confident with new people and although we initially had him muzzled for fear he would think that new people coming into the house were as in his last home; where he may have perceived them as a potential or actual threat (which would have previously been the case); it soon became apparent that this precaution was not necessary. He wags his tail for visitors and often goes over and gives them his paw, whilst craning his neck back for a stroke. He still continues to give first his left paw and then his right from a sitting position; accompanied by a wiggle of the tail and an imploring look if there is food available. He sits (without command) for treats, loves affection and this trick often goes down well, melting the hearts of visitors! If it doesn't, of course, they can leave! He started to come off the lead more and more and now comes off wherever we go. He is very attentive, always looking back to check where we are. It is much easier with him off the lead as his reaction to other dogs is absolutely fine off the lead. He is not a good ambassador for the breed when he is on the lead as he projects an inaccurate image. Although much better than he used to be, when on the lead, he would still tug and bark and seem half-crazed; but off the lead, he transforms into the perfect ambassador as he wags his tail, runs up to greet the fellow canine walker and often enjoys a bit of banter and fun with them. Sometimes, he charges over at full pelt which is reminiscent of Fleck's behaviour and the terror on the faces of the horrified owners only subsides when we start yelling his name in vain!

Occasionally, my heart would be in my mouth as during a walk, he could bark and rear up at joggers or cyclists coming towards him in the forest or park. Nevertheless, there was no aggression in him and this was more to do with defensiveness as he must think they are coming towards him to threaten him. As the weeks went on, however, this has worn off when out and about, and apart from the occasional bark, accompanied by tail wagging, when meeting other dogs, he was getting very sociable with new people, running over and flapping his tail in eager welcome.

Again, we muzzled him initially until one week we went for a walk with a friend and her greyhound Damson; and her rescued Galga, Lorelei. We realised we had left the muzzle at home and he was absolutely fine without it. Will loved running with Damson and Lorelei who are both remarkable dogs. Damson came from the kennels and Lorelei is rescued from Spain. The Galgo is the Spanish greyhound used in Spain for hunting and there are so many that need homes having suffered terrible abuse. When the hunting season ends, literally thousands of these poor dogs are abandoned. Some are hung from trees with bets placed on who will die first. Cruelty in the extreme can be inflicted on these sensitive dogs with them being abandoned in remote places with their legs broken; along with various other methods of dispatchment. Charities are doing their best to rescue as many as possible and find new homes across Europe, including in the UK. Lorelei is a beautiful dog who is so obedient and gentle and has proved herself to be wonderful in the home. Having Will off the lead was initially terrifying, but he needs it to run off some energy. I am so proud of him and he is less of a hooligan when off the lead. However, there have been a couple of moments when he forgets himself and becomes over-excited, leaping up and grabbing your sleeve as he thinks again that he is a working police-dog wrestling a convict to the ground!

His first friend off the lead was the black rescued spaniel, Sam. Sam remains as beautiful and friendly as ever, loving a game and charging over whenever he sees us in the forest.   As I said, when Will was on the lead, he would strain at the leash, barking at Sam for all he was worth. Now, he plays with him without any problem and enjoys running with every dog he meets. On one occasion, we met a Mexican Hairless Dog who was tiny and on the lead. Will went charging over and had a shock when the little thing turned and yapped, not wanting to join in with this brindle burst of energy. As we chatted to the owner, we commented on the fact that we had not seen such a breed before. It turns out the dog had been rescued and this just underlines the fact that there is every possible dog of every possible age in rescues and breed-specific rescues. No matter what the breed, there are centres where homeless animals are available. So many thousands of dogs need homes and homes are limited. For this reason, it underlines the importance of neutering because, apart from those few circumstances where breeding is responsible, every unwanted litter produced is unnecessary and means another rescued dog missing out on a home.

Will is a comical boy too. He makes me laugh and seems to resemble the canine version of 'Just William'. After he has been out for a while, he is oblivious to the fact that his rain coat is all skew-whiff and he emerges from the bushes with one ear forward and one ear folded back.

The way he gazes out of the kennel door if he accompanies me is always amusing as he pretends he has not seen you and gazes forward with a plaintive look, purposefully looking sad and confined. He knows you are looking but continues to express resigned boredom, head between his paws which are resting on the bars as he stands on his hind legs to look out. As you pass, he will paw you through the bars and look to the side, following you as you go down the passage. A look of hope and relief on his face as if to say: "good, it"s worked; time to go"! Stopping at his kennel will mean a little wiggle of the tail in anticipation and, after a reassuring kiss on the nose, he usually steals himself for a longer wait. Sometimes he can be noisy though as if he has not seen you or can see you nearby, he will scream and holler to make sure you haven't left him!

We also walk with three other dogs from the kennels: Fonzie, Charlie and Danny. Their adopter takes in old dogs and gives them the home they deserve in the twilight years of their life. Often these dogs have not been socialised and the years of being told to chase have meant they think this is still expected. However, after a few weeks in his care, they are off the lead without a muzzle, running with all sorts of other breeds and given a life they could never have imagined. Will loves to run free with them whenever we join them; as well as with their Yorkshire Terrier friends who were playing with a ball. The little dogs would tear after the ball and Will would join in the game, chasing along, but often overshooting the ball and running on! He would spend the whole walk running with all the dogs and would be utterly exhausted once he got home! Once, he decided it would be a good idea to roll in a cow pat; a smell that was even worse than the dreaded fox-poo! Although we had to endure this odour for the journey home, a quick rub with tomato ketchup and a bath quickly led to one damp, red, but clean dog.

We were all lucky to have Charlie with us. His rescue had overtones of Will's own rescue. He had been rehomed two years before and the couple were now unwell and the daughter wanted Charlie to be returned to the kennels (aged eleven years old). Charlie had been with us for quite a long time before he was rehomed as it had been told to us by his original owner that he would not be suitable to home with other greyhounds. It is always heart rending to see them come back, but especially emotional when they have to come back at such an age – and moreover, in the cold months of the year when they have been used to a warm home. Usually the dogs turn up on the allotted return day, but Charlie did not turn up as scheduled. Upon enquiry, the daughter informed us that he had been dropped off at the kennels a few days before; which of course, he had not. Where on earth was he? After a lot of phone calls, improvised detective work and worrying, we finally traced him to a council pound. By this stage, he had been offered a home so we all went to collect him from the pound. The journey ran smoothly until we missed our junction on the motorway.

We had to go to the next junction (which was, of course, miles away!), turn round and then retrace our steps as the other side did not have the same exits and junctions! Then our directions took us on a scenic route through the countryside! Whilst we would normally appreciate the rustic fresh air and enchanting thatched cottages, we just wanted to get to Charlie and our frustration was even more evident when we stopped to ask directions from someone we thought was a local; but who turned out to be very nice and attempted to help but was actually new to the area and hardly spoke English!

Eventually, however, we found the place, but not without the help of some long-term locals who very kindly guided us to the door. I saw Charlie from a distance being put back in his pen. He was oblivious to our presence and it was like watching a scene from a film. What a relief that we had found him. They handed him over and he had found his home at last. It turned out that he had been dumped across town. They could not even be bothered to make the journey back to the kennels so had turfed out an eleven year old dog who had trusted them and been settled for over two years. The confusion and betrayal these dogs must feel is unfathomable and yet still they put their trust in their new human companion. They are amazing animals and really are man's best friend, although we fail to live up to the loyalty they deserve.

Thankfully, that was Charlie in a wonderful home, but he wasn't the end of our rescue missions during our first couple of years of Will's return!

On the way to the kennels we were to encounter two more dogs that came across our path! One morning, I was on my way in the car and Will and Storm were accompanying me. Will had decided that he preferred to travel next to me. Will is so loving that he takes any opportunity to be next to me and get as near as he can! Will wanted to get closer so clambered into the front seat of the car, from the boot, over a bemused Storm in the back! The two boys had got over any differences and were now getting along fine. As Will curled up in the passenger seat, I thanked goodness that we were in a quiet lane, very near to the kennels and early in the morning. Otherwise, I would have had to get out and re-arrange them! What would we look like as we rolled up at the kennels! Will sat there looking out of the window, although it was quite dark so there was not a lot to see!

Famous last words of course! Just ahead, there was something white, running along the edge of the road. Oh no, not again!

The Jack Russell was definitely unattended and as we got closer, it was clear that he was quite scruffy. Surely this could not be another stray. Would I have to go home and present mum with a Jack Russell now!? I stopped the car, grabbed a slip-lead, turned on the hazard lights and jumped out. As I approached, the dog scooted off to the left and I suddenly panicked, doubting if I had shut the car door! There could now potentially be three dogs needing to be rounded up! I turned round and whizzed back to the car. Thankfully Storm and Will were just sitting there, watching me run up and down! I locked the door and ran back to the Jack Russell. He came towards me, but something spooked him and he darted off again. He disappeared into a nearby yard and, as I followed him in, he ran towards a metal door and ducked under the small gap and vanished. He must live on the site! So that was ok!

It wasn't long before another dog was found wandering in the lane, but thankfully he also lived in the house nearby. They must spot our car and plan a hijack attempt!

The next dog to fall into our hands was a Labrador called Fudge who was ambling towards us through a housing estate through which we pass on our way to the kennels. He was clearly on his own so once again, I pulled over and stopped the car. The car was completely full that day. Storm was in the back, Will was in the boot and mum in the passenger seat. In the foot-wells of the car, food for the forty dogs at the kennels was rammed – their treat which was cooked on a Saturday and mixed with the tinned food, which was packed in around the tubs.

I followed the Labrador as it passed the houses. He was heading for the forest and so I called him, knowing that if he started to weave between the trees, he would be lost from sight and probably from potential recovery. He came rushing over, but I was unprepared and did not have a lead. Suddenly, I spied a man with three Labradors on a lead. This must be the owner. I yelled over, but he was not missing a dog. He was a local dog walker and verified that the dog was not from the immediate vicinity as he had not seen this dog before.

"You'll have to take him," he said.

How on earth was I supposed to fit him in an already full-to-bursting micra? But what else could I do? The kennels has a micro-chip scanner so if we could just get him there, we may be able to get him home quickly. I did not dare to think what would happen or what we would do with him if he was not chipped.

The dog walker stood guard while I ran back to the car to get a lead. I am no Usain Bolt, always having been the slowest in my class at school, but I could have given him a run for his money that day! Thankfully, the Labrador stayed with the other dogs and I got the lead over him. I realised quickly that it would be foolish to put him in the back with Storm; so he would have to travel in the front passenger seat. Will looked on incredulously from his third class 'boot' position, but there was nothing else for it! There was no way that mum's new hip was going to tolerate being rammed in the back with Storm and being contorted over pots of pasta. Mum would have to drive; and I would travel with my legs at awkward angles in the back with Storm; balancing between tins of dog food and twisted around the pasta. After a very uncomfortable journey (for me!) where I would have paid any number of speeding fines just to get there more quickly, we made it. The Labrador, by contrast, had a luxurious ride, looking out of the window and enjoying the passing scenery. To our total relief, he was chipped and it was revealed that he had recently been adopted from the rescue kennel down the lane! The owner's grand-daughter came along to collect him; and not before time. He spent the whole time standing in the paddock, barking his lungs off until someone came to see him! He was absolutely lovely, but there was no way mum was going to agree to have him so we would have been totally stuck if he had not been claimed!

We had a similar incident in our local forest when we recovered a lone black Labrador. We walked him to the vet and found him to be chipped. His owner had turned up in floods of tears, so full of relief that his boy had been found.

With so many animals ending up in pounds; and so many healthy dogs put to sleep through lack of space, estimated at twenty dogs per day in the UK alone, it is good news that the microchips prevented these dogs ending up back in the system to await their fate.

It does seem that animals have a way of finding their way to those who will help them. We've had ducks with their babies walking by; swans landing in front of us; lame and mangy foxes seeking sanctuary (and with the help of some mange-treatment, being restored to full health); birds landing in our porch (when they had the option of one hundred other houses on our road); and even a Polish homing pigeon whose navigating techniques were clearly not up to scratch! However, it is always a joy to see an animal restored to health or helped if you can do what you can to come to its aid. Treating a fox and seeing the mange clear up, fur re-grow and the fox no longer scratching itself to pieces is very satisfying as it is a little bit of suffering relieved and that individual can go on its way to lead a happier and more fulfilled life.

Walking in the forest, we have now made four new friends: Cecil, Cyril, Cedric and Celia (or so we have named them). These crows follow us as we walk the well-trod trail around the forest. They see us when we come in and fly over, waiting on their strategic perches at various points around our path as we pass by. They will land behind us, cawing; awaiting their seed which they know is coming their way. They recognise us from a long distance away and other walkers have looked quizzically as we are pursued by the strange quartet during our walk!

Will, off the lead as he always is now, will engage in bouts of chasing as Cecil (or Celia, or even Cedric and Cyril) land, but it is more about running at them than any serious attempt to catch them. They are never in any danger as they nonchalantly lift themselves into the air out of harm's way, before making their way to their next vantage point. Will, meanwhile runs on. His speed is very impressive and it is a wonderful sight to see him running free, loving his energy bursts while enjoying the sniffs and smells of whatever path takes his fancy. He is reliable with all other breeds and although his tendency of rushing over madly, remains; he does not show any aggression and will often wander off if the other dog is too rough. He did receive a taste of his own medicine, however, when he encountered 'Chunky' – a huge mastiff-type dog who is very friendly and loves greyhounds. We did not tell Chunky that Will is actually a lurcher so it was a very animated mastiff that Will joined when he went charging over. We were then witness to the very comical scene of Will turning on his heels and being pursued himself in a very amiable game of chase where Will was, for once, the one running away! Dear old Storm stays on the lead as we do not trust his recall. Although Storm is good with most dogs, he is also not terribly friendly with a Welsh Collie called Jojo (the feeling is mutual), but the possibility of an encounter with this dog precludes the possibility of him being allowed to roam free.

Chapter Twelve:

"We are going to call her Blobby"

Six months after Fleck's death, the kennels took in a batch of ten greyhounds from a holding kennel. They arrived on a Monday morning and as the van rolled up, I grabbed a pen and paper to make a note of where they were going so we would not get the names confused. As the dogs were unloaded, it was clear that they were all different characters. They had all previously been paired up so were put in the paddocks with the companion with whom they would be sharing their kennel. They were relieved to be out after their journey and ran around, stretching their legs and enjoying their freedom. They were all confident and happy, wagging their tails, enjoying the affection they were receiving and returning it in bucket loads. All but one of the dogs was black. Black is a colour which is often overlooked in rescues. Whether it is dogs or cats, black animals tend to be second in preference to the more obvious colours. It is an absolute travesty and more needs to be done to raise their profile and promote their wonderful characteristics.

"Next one out is Patti – she's quite nervous; she goes in with Paul," said the driver.

"I'll come out with you," I said.

In one of the carrier crates was a little black female with a scar on her nose where she had obviously been wearing a muzzle. It had clearly cut into her and whoever had 'looked after' her had not removed it. The whites of her eyes were showing and she was shaking with fear. As she was lifted out, she must have wondered where on earth she was going and what was about to happen to her. I put her in the paddock with Paul and she was clearly relieved to see him. She cowered away from me as I brought her some dinner. These reactions speak volumes. She had clearly been abused and, upon reading the notes which accompanied the dogs from the holding kennel, they said she had arrived to them in a terrible state and had to have her strength built up for a while before she was well enough to be spayed. She was eight years old and had run 150 races, a number which is far too many in my opinion. She was terribly nervous, suggesting a traumatic history at the kennels of those for whom she had run. However, you could also see a playful side coming out and a very loving girl as she started to trust us.

Storm really needed a friend again and although he and Will now get along, like us, he was still really missing Fleck. Fleck would always be in our thoughts, but perhaps the time had come where we could think of her looking down, pleased that we could offer her space to another needy soul who would benefit from a loving home. Fleck's toy, 'Purple,' an unidentifiable toy creature which is something like a cross between an alien and a hippo is a treasured item of sentimental value with which she is pictured in a lovely photograph. As mum said, however, she left her toys for others to play with and I like to think that in the future when, as the poems state, we are all reunited, all those who have played with it will reflect on a shared history, albeit at different times (if Purple can survive the rough shakings and be played with for that long, of course!).

Despite this philosophical attitude from mum, I was not convinced that she would ever agree to a third dog! I still had to work on this one! Surely she would come round!? Patti, however, really needed a home. The holding kennel had said she wore a little coat at night and liked to snuggle into it. She was eight years old, nervous and black; hardly the easiest to home. Perhaps we could be the ones to give her the chance of a life in the warm with some love. Two weeks went by so I knew I had to turn up the pressure!

Mum finally relented after I left notes around the house (as I had done for Fleck) and when I put Patti in the paddock with Will and Storm on a Sunday morning while all the volunteers cheered her on!! Patti was fine with Will and Storm and they stayed out together all morning. In typical 'mother' fashion, she agreed in public, but once we were alone in private she started turning on the negatives:

"Oh I don't know, I don't want this" etc.

Yet, she had just said 'yes'!

Anyway, eventually, my long-suffering mother agreed to take her on the Monday. There was still doubt in my mind that she would agree so I did not allow myself to get too excited. I could not think she would agree and then be disappointed.

I went to the kennels as usual on the Monday morning, starting at 7.30am and staying until 4pm. It is a very long day as you are on your feet all day and walking about all the time. Invariably, people arrive as soon as you sit down, which means you have to get straight back up again! Of course, this is always a good thing as we want potential visitors to adopt dogs, but it can be exhausting! Mum comes up at 1pm to join me and when she arrived that day, I waited for the gate to click. However, she took ages to come in! Eventually, I wandered towards the gate and found her talking to the lady from the kennel next door. She had a wry smile on her face and was talking about how we are going to have Patti! It's like she does, yet does not want to have her! Either way, she could not back out of it now!

When we left, I took Patti in my car while Storm and Will went with mum. I thought she may be less worried if she was with me as she knew me a bit more.

We made it home without incident and she was fine with Will and Storm. I had already sneakily tested her with our Humphrey the cat and she had passed this test – just! The first night, she did mess in the house, but she got the hang of it and quickly learnt that the garden is the place for that. You cannot blame her after a lifetime in kennels. When she paces around, we let her in the garden and know this is the time for toilet breaks! They adapt so very quickly and are amazingly adaptable to new circumstances. They are far less work than other breeds and much less work than a puppy who needs constant house-training! We always say that you may get an accident on the first night because they do not know the routine, but it is rare for this to continue; and many are clean from the start.

She was absolutely petrified of every new sound or any movement. A simple raising of the arms to reach something, or even putting her food bowl down would invoke a reaction from cowering, shaking or simply showing the whites of her eyes in fear. She would jump out of her skin at the most insignificant of things which we would take for granted. After a couple of weeks, however, her playful side began to show and she would wag her tail when we came downstairs to them in the morning.

She would scoot around the garden, blundering about in a strange way which typified her nervous energy. She always goes dashing into the garden, before running back up the steps to the back door for reassurance. Over the first two months, she really started to improve and gain in confidence. She really took to Will and absolutely loves his company. Poor old Storm, with whom we had hoped she would form a bond, was ok to hang around with, but Will was the one she followed. She started to pick up and learn from him. This was sod's law - why could she not learn from Storm's calming influence?! Thankfully, the barking was the one exception to this education! She charges in the garden and even starts mouthing your hand when it is time to put the lead on. However, she is the most gentle dog and you can do anything with her in the knowledge that she will not react. We would trust her with a baby! She is not a push-over though as she still stands her ground if Storm and Will get too close to her bed. She revels in the comforts of the soft dog bed, snuggling into the cosiness of the warmth and softness – presumably two things that she would have experienced little before in her life.

Strangely, it took me a while to pluck up the courage to put one of Fleck's coats on her. It was still too painful to see them, but in the meantime, I was given a coat which was surplus to requirements at the kennels. Written on it, was the name of its former wearer: Blobby. Who on earth called a poor dog that?! The best names are the old fashioned names in my opinion. Some of the best are: Trevor, George, Betty, Rodney! Can you imagine the christening: "we're going to call her: Blobby". Of course, whilst Patti remains Patti (or Pattiricia/Patricia), when we are in a silly mood, she is occasionally called Blobby; as everyone has silly names for their dogs! Or is that just us!?

Within the first two weeks, she had to get used to two men who were coming and going in order to renovate our cloakroom and garage. One of them had actually adopted a greyhound recently from the kennels and both were more than happy to work around the dogs. Patti was initially very frightened, but it was good to have her face her fears as she showed a fantastic change after just a couple of weeks. At the start, she had run away if they came in, but after two weeks, she would stay on her bed, come into the room if they were in there and even let them stroke her. She absolutely loves her toys and carries them around, often coming running to the door when we come in carrying a fluffy chicken, her string of plastic sausages or her fluffy rabbit. She likes to bring them all into the lounge with us and throw them around, hurling them in the air across the room, pouncing on them and scattering them about. She is a very loveable dog with a fantastic personality which is showing itself more and more as she relaxes and enjoys the comforts of the security of having a home. Her affectionate nature is revealing itself too as she comes up excitedly for a cuddle, even barging the boys out of the way at times!

Storm remains a gentle and simple soul who loves affection and gets very excited when he goes for a walk. When he is asked if he 'wants to go walking'?, he goes running down the hall and flails his legs around in enthusiasm. He walks like a dressage horse when he is pleased and looks very grand indeed! It's a shame that he does not always understand the logistics of walking round trees on a lead (and often has to be unravelled), but he really is such a fabulous boy. He has started to learn from Will and sort-of raises his front paw when we need to clean them after a walk. He will lay on the floor and put his paw out and up for more tummy rubs and cuddles, leaning his head onto your arm as you sit with him on the floor.

It's a shame for Storm that Patti loves Will so much as it was Storm who was most missing Fleck. Will remains devoted to me and continues to be an incredible dog. He has now employed the doleful expression at home as well as at the kennels; as he stares over the baby-gate, resting his head on it and resenting our attempts to contain him while the cats eat. Often, of course, he will not let it beat him, jumping over to find me! We can touch his tummy now and he will join me wherever I am, often lying across me or beside me with his head on my knee or lap. He even clambers into the arm-chair when mum is out and makes himself at home in the smallest of spaces. His soppiness and 'rolling over' onto his back, legs akimbo, continues and many lurcher and greyhound owners will recognise this in their own dogs. However, there is nothing like the personal relationship of love that each unique individual human experiences with their unique individual furry friend.

It was now difficult for me to transport all three in my micra! However, this obstacle was overcome when Will once again sat in the front seat. Will sat in the passenger seat, Storm in the back and Patti in the boot. They all travel very well, as most greyhounds do, and just sit down all the way. It was highly amusing to see Will nonchalantly curled up in the passenger seat as he had the previous time he had invaded that space on the way up the lane! On the one longer journey I undertook with the three dogs in these positions, I watched him as he initially had to work out whether it was best to sit with his head by the window or by the gear. Eventually he sorted himself out and worked out how to sit on his side. On the return journey, he immediately sat still in the preferred position as he had remembered the best way to travel.

Patti had not met any other breeds before she came to us (as far as we know). She passed the cat-test, but we need to be careful with initial introductions to other breeds as sometimes she thinks she is still expected to chase them! We are still careful with the cats too as she must have played her cards right at the initial test just to disguise the reality that she can be slightly temperamental with them!

Humphrey the cat is the initial cat-tester and most of the recent greyhounds homed with cats have met him. The dogs come into the house muzzled and on a lead and we gauge their reaction when Humphrey walks down the hall. We can quickly tell the dogs that are not going to pass the test and the dogs that are going to be fine (always with total precautions being taken). However, those who are fifty-fifty are always more difficult to judge. Humphrey is very good as he always gives them a bash with his paw and this puts the greyhounds in their place as well as startling them. They are used to small animals running away from them, but Humphrey standing up to them makes them acknowledge that they are not in charge! It always amuses me when the greyhounds are scared of Humphrey and start hiding behind my knees or looking away in trepidation, pretending he is not there!

Humphrey is facing retirement due to his increasing frailty, so our other cat, Molly, is due to take on this role. She is not likely to be so good at it being a bit more of a 'scardy-cat' but hopefully she will relish the role (...unlikely!). She can be quite daft and, despite being over eight years old, is still called 'the kitten' due to her baby-like behaviour. Our neighbours are having their bungalow converted into a house so the scaffolding is covering the house. Molly must be the only cat that would ever get stuck on it and be unable to get down.

"Where's Molly? I can hear a mewing", said mum.

"She's out somewhere".

"Oh dear – she's stuck on the scaffolding – where are the step-ladders, we are going to have to go up there and get her down"!

As we attempted to clamber up from our side of the fence, we realised there was no way we could do it from the back garden. We would have to attempt it from the front of the house. There have been quite a few burglaries in the area so our clandestine efforts to climb onto someone else's property could be cause for the local constabulary to descend upon us! We managed to position the steps against the edge of the scaffolding and as I ascended, Molly was still mewing.

"Molly", I hissed in a stage whisper.

Her little face appeared and as she came towards us, the security light came on!

"Good evening", said a voice.

"Hello", we both replied in unison, trying to sound as jovial and natural as possible so he would not suspect us of illegal activity. It is amazing how guilty you feel when you are actually totally innocent! It was the neighbour from further down the road, coming home late.

He clearly felt it was quite normal for us to be up a step-ladder on our neighbour's property at midnight!

Chapter 13:

"Nobody can fully understand the meaning of love unless he's owned a dog" (Gene Hill)

Getting to know each unique individual animal is always a thrill. This is seen so prominently at the kennels where each individual is different, with their own character, wants and needs. Each one is special and irreplaceable and bonding with them is a real joy. Of course, some stick in your mind more forcefully than others, as do some owners! The variety of human visitors never ceases to astound. As already said, you see both extremes of humanity: those who love, care and have respect and compassion for the dogs versus those who do not. Things are also not always as they seem and sometimes it is those who express it less gushingly who sometimes actually have more genuine passion and care. Some potential adopters are of course, totally unsuitable due to their home set-up or their feelings towards animals. Others have fantastic lifestyles where the chosen dog really falls on their paws.

Jinxy was one of those lucky dogs. She had been a racing dog and initially been taken home by her racing owner. After a while, they decided to move house and did not want to take Jinxy with them. She came into the kennels at the coldest time of the year and was overlooked for a few months. One day, after a busy day, I went to the vet to pick up a dog after its neutering operation. Usually I am in-and-out in less than five minutes, but on this particular occasion, I had to wait for their computer to finish a print-job before I could pay our bill. This meant I returned to the kennels later than anticipated and was late in closing up. Thankfully, I was still on the site when Fergie and Pye's owner turned up to collect a bottle of medicine. He wanted to look at the dogs and wandered up the corridor, saying 'hello' to each dog.

"Are there any that can live with small dogs"? he asked.

"Well, there is Jinxy", I responded tentatively! The family already had three dogs. Was he really serious? I couldn't push them!

But Jinxy really deserved a chance and had proven to be good with other breeds when out and about on a walk in the local park.

"I think i've fallen in love with her", he said; as Jinxy immediately jumped up at him as if she had found her owner! "Let me ring my wife"!

He took Jinxy home there and then! It also turned out that the family have four and a half acres for a garden – so what a wonderful life she has there!

Then there are dogs who are returned to the kennels through no fault of their own. This is always the saddest thing as they know home-life and are then enclosed again in a small kennel without home comforts or the love they have (should have) enjoyed. Of course, we insist they come back to the kennels if ever circumstances change so this option is the only one and we are always glad they come back safely and are not passed on elsewhere. One of these dogs was Fonzie, one of Will's new friends. He had lived in a home for four years with another dog called Trudy. Both were returned to the kennels and we had to pick them up from their home. Fonzie was quite strong, but an absolutely beautiful and affectionate dog. When we picked him up from the home, he came running to the door with his toy. It was absolutely heartbreaking to have to put him in the car and take him back to the kennels. He fretted terribly, but at least he had Trudy with him.

They were taken for a day out at a local school one afternoon when another of our adopters had set aside a talk about pets. Fonzie and Trudy were wonderful with the children; waiting patiently while a talk was given and then allowing people to stroke them and ask questions.

A few weeks later, a woman rang wanting a pair and we were so hopeful because Fonzie and Trudy now had a chance. They went off home together, both wearing huge over-sized green coats because it was pouring with rain! But devastatingly, they were returned after a couple of weeks due to unexpected circumstances. We were not sure if the lady wanted to give them another chance and so they stayed in the kennel for a few more weeks. Fonzie was getting increasingly stressed back in kennels and it was very distressing to see him chewing the bed boards in his frustration. He was out in the paddocks one day when he was running with Trudy; and accidentally, he caught her skin, causing a bite wound. This meant he now had to be split from Trudy.

Trudy was subsequently collected by the woman who had previously offered the pair a home and this meant good news for Trudy. But Fonzie was in the kennels, still looking for a home. I felt so sorry for him as he had lost his owner, his home, his home-life; and now his buddy. It was good that Trudy had found a caring home, but Fonzie was getting increasingly desperate. I had grown very fond of him and wanted to ensure that whoever homed him would love him now as he deserved.

One day, a retired couple came to the kennels and chose him. It all seemed wonderful, but when we did the re-check, Fonzie had lost a lot of weight and it transpired that they had not been feeding him enough. This was not deliberate cruelty, but seems to be a common mistake as people assume that greyhounds are thin dogs and that this must mean the bones must show. This, however, is categorically not the case. The outline of a few ribs should be seen, but they should not be poking out! The two pin-bones at the top of the back hips should also not be poking out. Moreover, when the dogs are retired, they should also weigh more than their stream-lined racing weight.

We offered advice, but sadly Fonzie was later returned to the kennels. Once again, his distress levels escalated and it was so sad to witness. On one particular occasion, the kennels became over-run with dogs and the kennel owner had to resort to fostering some dogs out to accommodate everyone! Fonzie went to a long term adopter who had had over thirty dogs in his lifetime and took the older dogs who are likely to be overlooked. There were already two other boys at home, but Fonzie was taken on a temporary basis. The adopter worked wonders with the dogs and even those who want to chase after anything small and furry, including smaller dogs, were re-trained and socialised very quickly. Fonzie was eight years old and it was initially felt that this was still young enough for Fonzie to go back to the kennels after the fostering period. However, the adopter's opinion quickly changed when he grew so attached to him and decided to give him a permanent home!! It is an amazing home for Fonzie who is now off the lead, good with other dogs and had at last found his 'forever home'.

Whisky, a black dog with white flashes, is another dog who fell on his feet after three previous homes. He had been brought back twice due to the new adopters failing to take on board the advice of the kennels. He was then adopted by a wonderfully doting, kind elderly couple who worshipped him. The husband did all the walking as the lady had had a stroke. They came to all the kennels' events and loved Whisky to pieces. Tragically, the husband had a heart-attack and had to go into hospital; meaning Whisky had to come into the kennels to be looked after as the lady could not cope. Whisky was quite distressed and was slobbering in his kennel, chewing the bars and generally getting very anxious. The situation then worsened when the elderly couple were unable to have Whisky back due to both their declining health. This was one example where nobody was to blame and it was just as devastating for us to hear the sorrow of the two owners as it was to see the plight of Whisky. They were crying down the phone and so very upset. It was so very sad for all involved, but they had absolutely no choice so had to put Whisky's welfare first. Whisky was therefore back permanently again and it seemed his luck had run out.

Our hopes were raised again when he was reserved by a lady with a child; and we were so relieved that he would go quickly. She was so enthusiastic, but bizarrely, he was returned one week later. As I've said before, we always want the dogs to come back to us if they cannot be kept, but sometimes it is very frustrating. Whisky was back yet again, and, like Fonzie, his stress levels spiralled.

When he was at his wits end, there was a light at the end of the tunnel for him. A lovely couple who had sadly lost their dog, came along to adopt again as their other dog was pining and needed a friend. They decided to give Whisky a chance and he found his 'forever' home there.

There are countless other examples, each of whom could have a book in their own right: Molly, an older black (going grey) girl, who was with us for over a year (and who came in with Patti in the batch of ten) was a real character who loved a game and stuck her head out of the door of the kennel to lick passers by. Famous for her buck-toothy smile, she was a favourite with many people and struck lucky when a family with a greyhound and a galgo saw her on an 'oldies' website. There was Rebel, a lovely black dog who just seemed to 'stick' in the kennels and was a real long-termer, who then found a fabulous home where he is idolised and has proven himself to be impeccable at home. Princess, was another character who had not raced and was a real bundle of fun and naughtiness. She was returned once and stayed in the kennels for ages waiting, until a very kind couple who had a Staffie which they had adopted as the longest-stay dog in the kennels, wanted to adopt a long-stay girl. Princess now lives by the sea and has bonded very well with the Staffie. Then there was Jake, one dog I particularly bonded with, who had been with a trainer who was struck-off for abusing dogs, and found a home with two of the home-checkers. Jake did not always take to everyone whilst in the kennels, probably due to his history, but he was so loyal and affectionate once he got to know you and I always looked forward to seeing him in the mornings. He has adapted fantastically well at home and we still get to see him sometimes too!

Despite all the sadness that went before, these are the outcomes that make it so worthwhile.

Of course, this feeling never leaves me when I look at Will. Everyone said to me: "you can't save them all" and this may be true, but it should not mean we do not try. We can save the individuals who we know about and who cross our path. I could not live with myself if I had not tried. Sometimes, we cannot be successful, but if we do not try, we will never know. And sometimes our efforts will pay off. No matter what the outcome, the good we do can never be for nothing as if it has the potential to succeed, we could be the mechanism for securing a better life for one special and unique individual.

Getting Will back was an amazing experience as the relief that he is ok has lifted the guilt and constant worry from my shoulders. He is no longer suffering and we now have an unbeatable bond. He is a wonderful boy and we are so lucky to have him back with us. He is safe and will not know the sadness of being unwanted again; additionally, of course, he has also enriched our lives immensely. Yes, his initial weeing, pulling on the lead and crying at night were things we had not experienced with our other dogs. This little lunatic was a hooligan compared with Storm and Fleck, who were so easy that we hardly knew they were there, but he is a fantastic dog who has found his place at last.

Each has their own character and Patti has now added her own zest to the crew. She is a funny little dog with her habits of lying across beds, digging them into a ball, flopping down in satisfaction and yet sitting mainly on the floor, copying Will and flying around the garden despite her older years and her funny way of being excited, yet running in the opposite direction when we announce we are "going walking". So far, she has only been to the vet for her routine vaccinations so apart from the odd grazes from her exertions, she is clearly not as accident prone as Fleck!

Will still gets very exuberant when we 'go walking'. We like to take them to different areas for a different walk now and again and he never fails to amuse. One particular location requires a ticket for the car for parking. Will always can barely contain himself as he waits, watching in the car as we put the coins into the machine. He leaps from the boot into the back with a bemused Storm and then flies over into the front of the car, peering out from the drivers seat as if he has been responsible for driving the party to the scene! He is friendly with everyone, but still looks to me for reassurance at times. He once left the allocated path and wandered onto a golf course. We called him back, but heard a yelp and he came running back to my side, gazing up at me and rubbing his head and body along my leg for comfort.

Storm has sadly not been well recently. Despite numerous tests and scans, nothing can be detected and it has been assumed he has had a stroke. He has several vets totally baffled! He even stopped urinating for three weeks and heavy clouds hung in our heart as we felt we were going to have to make a decision. However, scans showed his organs were functioning normally (albeit with a slight kidney issue) and that his bladder was emptying of its own volition through 'dripping'. Of course, this pleased mum enormously when he wandered around the house, meaning we had to keep him contained in just two rooms which we smothered with incontinence pads. Thank goodness we do not operate a home-run business! Like a miracle, he went into the garden one morning and started weeing. I had to do a double take! He has continued ever since!

He is slightly slower than he used to be, both on the uptake as well as physically. He is the dearest dog and his coat has gone fluffy, making him even more cuddly! It has also turned a pale grey – he's a mystery!

He can still join us on walks and we all joined another adopted 'kennel-dog' called Quest for a party to celebrate Quest's 'year-at-home'! The dogs love to meet with other greyhounds and it is so nice for Will to continue his socialising with others too!

Two days later, Will gave us a terrible fright when he suddenly developed horrendous bloody diarrhoea. I was panic stricken and when he continued with this through the evening, we rushed him to the local veterinary hospital, fearing something dreadful was going on inside him. Thankfully, the vet was not so panic-stricken and felt that he had eaten something which had caused this gastric trouble.

Unlike Patti, he appears to have taken on Fleck's role as accident attractor! The next veterinary visit happened quickly afterwards when he hurt himself in the garden and sustained a wound which demanded antibiotics and veterinary attention. His side swelled up like a tennis ball and he had to be put on the table at the surgery and have it drained. I was worried he would have to have an anaesthetic, but thankfully, it was felt a drain could be inserted to allow any residue to clear; and hopefully this would solve it. Will would have to wear a buster-collar so did a very good impression of Little Bo Peep for a few days, crashing into things to try and get the bonnet off his head. In the end we put a muzzle on him instead and stuck a coat on him to cover the wound so he could not pull out the drains in his side. He continued to charge into anything (legs, sofas, gates) to try to remove the muzzle, but overall, this seemed to take his mind off the issue and the wound gradually healed, although some scar tissue has left a small swelling on his side after the drain was removed.

Unfortunately, he did not learn his lesson from this escapade and remains poised to run when he stands at the back door. If anyone doubts that the poise of an athlete at the start of a race can help to speed them up at the beginning, they should take a look at Will's posture as he gets ready to race out of the door, front paws bent, body pushed back, bottom and tail in the air as he gets ready to propel himself forward at top speed in the hope of spying any foxes who might be hanging out in the garden! Due to this speed and obsession, we used to put a muzzle on him when he goes out for his late evening toilet break - just in case!

Horrifically, he ran outside one night and collapsed in the garden. It had been quite wet and the ground was muddy so he may well have slipped, but we do not know for sure. He was screaming on the ground, flailing around with his front legs and unable to move his back legs. Were they broken? I rushed to him and he was panicking, distressed and stuck. I felt his legs and spine and could not feel any obvious breaks or see any swelling. I was screaming and panicking myself and mum rushed out to see what all the commotion was about. It was dark and late so she was conscious that the neighbours might be alarmed. I could not have cared less what they thought! I was just concerned about Will's legs. Thoughts of Magic and Olive, two dogs at the kennels whose legs had collapsed due to an aneurysm and who had not made it were filling my head and I clung onto Will in distress. I tried to scoop him up, but his legs would not hold him and, in his panic he was lashing out and causing himself to fall backwards. It was a good thing he had the muzzle on! He was in so much pain and was crying and screaming. We let him go back down onto the grass and rest for a moment. He lay there and looked up at me with his eyes full of fear. I leant down to him and cuddled him. His front legs remained unaffected and he started giving me his paw from where he was laying. He does this in normal circumstances too. If he forgets himself, he can sometimes let out a warning growl. However, he knows this is unnecessary and immediately leaves the sofa, giving his paw to say sorry in acknowledgement that he did not mean it. He is always so respectful if Storm is on the sofa or bed and never attempts to move Storm on. He is a gentle, intelligent boy and even in this state was aware of his behaviour.

We managed to stand Will up on a sheet and support his legs, still unable to support themselves. We carried him back to the house and laid him down on a bed in the kitchen. I was grief-stricken and could not believe this was happening. No, please, no. He was really stressed, eyes rolling, panting and gasping and still unable to stand. After about half an hour on the floor with him, he calmed sufficiently for us to have another go at coaxing him to stand. After several attempts, where he kept flopping backwards and rocking around, he managed to support himself on one back leg. The other was dragging along the ground and, as he tried to walk, he fell again, collapsing backwards onto the bed. He could not raise his curly tail in the air; and it hung limply against his back legs.

As one leg seemed to be regaining some strength, we helped him into the sitting room, where I slept on the sofa all night. Mum joined me on the armchair, showing that despite all her misgivings, she now loves Will and was really concerned about him. He tried to get up in the night and let out a high pitched scream, but he managed to support himself enough for him to stagger, wobbling onto the patio to go to the toilet.

It was utterly devastating and emotionally draining. He was getting some strength back and the following morning was able to wag his tail once, before awkwardly sitting back on the bed. We phoned the vet and they were able to fit him in that morning. Before we left, he started to regain some strength and the relief that flooded into my terrified heart was overwhelming. The vet assured us that he could feel no breaks and suspected that he had slipped in his enthusiasm to get into the garden and twisted his spine or pulled his muscles. At the time of writing, Will is continuing to recover. He is on a 'no-walk' regime for a week as well as painkillers. He can wag his tail again and has started to run down the hall when he sees the postman, albeit at a slight drunken-slant. He is able to join me on the sofa again and remains strong when he wants to go out for a toilet break.

Hopefully he is on the way back to his previous self. He likes to sit with me wherever I am so is not happy that he cannot do the stairs at the moment. He cannot join me when I take Storm and Patti out so stays with mum. He is so pleased when we get back, but has endeared himself to Mum unlike never before. This is so much so that when the dogs were lying down, she came in, doing comic-dancing to the radio, entertaining them as she did so! Storm looked up and looked away again, resigned to strange behaviour. Patti looked horror-struck and Will was staggered and bemused by such madness!

Will is so loveable, so loyal and utterly devoted to me. He deserves all the love in the world and I am just as much of a devotee to him! He is an incredible dog who despite everything, remains friendly, loving and never ceases to make you laugh and keep you entertained by his antics. He is good off the lead and with other dogs and on top of this, I feel safe when he is around, thanks to knowing he would defend me if there was any problem. All my dogs are the most loyal friends you can have – a definition by which our human friends, for the most part and with the exception of only a few, fail astronomically to live up to by comparison. As soppy as it sounds, we are devoted to each other and our lives have become part of each other. Each animal is irreplaceable and the love and bond we share is irreplaceable.

Will has now taken to squeezing onto the sofa into the smallest gap (or against you if you lie with him on the floor). He will curl up, put his front paws on your lap and gaze up at you, trying to get as close as possible. Once you put your arms round him, his contentment is magnified and he leans into you, rolling onto his back, stretching his front legs up in the air and his back legs out. After he goes all soppy, he then snuggles into you. He really is the most loving and affectionate boy and I love him to bits. The way he gazes at you with his head on your knee; the way he will lay straight on his back next to me, with his head on my arm and his paw stretched out in my hand. Sometimes he will go silly and pull his ears down over his head with his paws before rolling on his back and stretching out flat! The bond is incredible; and he also tries to sit on my lap if there is no space on the sofa. Storm might be sitting next to me but Will will want to join us too! He tries to get on by standing on my lap, but this is not the best option for a comfy sleep so I often move over for him. He squeezes into a tiny gap and flops down, sometimes squashing me and putting his head on my lap, happy just to be with you. It can necessitate sticking his head up over the arm-rest, but that is fine as it means he has found his perch! When he gets off the sofa, he always does his exercises and stretches his back legs flat against the seat in a pose any yoga professional would be proud of. Of course, if he enacts his flexibility whilst I am on the sofa, my legs can bear the brunt of this routine.

Again, it sounds very mushy and although I rarely express it verbally, in truth I idolise him and am very protective! He has suffered so much and is such a wonderful boy. I said to mum that if all lurchers are like this, we must always have a lurcher. I'm not sure she jumped in agreement! "Hooligan Will" has come a long way though. He no longer barks at the bell on QI or the drum beat on adverts for "I'm a Celebrity Get me out of Here." He is consistently friendly and affectionate with visitors, running up and wagging his tail; giving his paw and sitting for them. I suspect he will always alert us to the fact of a fox being in the garden and treat us to sing-song howling at night; but he is the most fantastic dog, my great and loyal friend and it is so good to be in his company. If I go upstairs to my computer, he will charge up there to sit by me (and when mum is not looking, he is welcome to sit on my bed). If I have been out, he now always jumps up for a cuddle, putting both front paws on my shoulders with pleasure. Even if we pop out, he is always jubilant to see us and twitches his feet with pleasure, tail wagging frantically. If only he had not had to suffer for those two years. What he endured is too much to bear and we missed out on those two years which we could have spent together.

There are so many greyhounds, lurchers, pedigree dogs and 'all-sorts' dogs in rescues and pounds; needing love and having so much love to give. They are taken to centres or dumped at all ages and so often pedigree puppies will also be waiting to be adopted. There are such numbers of dogs desperate for homes and facing potential death due to lack of homes. Will could have been another statistic and disappeared into this number. Over 13,478 greyhounds need homes every year in England and Wales alone. They are such wonderful animals and if everyone knew how easy greyhounds were to look after, every home would be craving to adopt one! Every one of this number is a special creature, an individual with a life of their own. Each has its own unique uniqueness in its very being which should be encountered with care and a concern for its welfare. No matter how many brindle greyhounds there are in this world, there is only one Will and only one of all the others.

I sometimes think of the poor Staffie that lived with Will. I wonder what ever happened to him or her. Perhaps someone has stepped in to help him/her; or perhaps no one has helped and he/she is in a rescue centre or has been put to sleep along with the many other thousands of its breed in this country that never find loving homes. Or perhaps he/she is suffering somewhere. This is where action is so important and individuals can make a difference in the lives of individuals. Many inspiring people achieve remarkable things way beyond most of us; but perhaps they can lead us to do something for individuals about whom we know about. Humans can cause so much pain and suffering, but it is possible also to make the world a better place. It certainly rings true that 'evil flourishes when good people do nothing' and this is a lesson we should all take. We need to remember that helping one might not change the situation for the whole universe or issue, but it will change the world for that one individual. Even if the world is made just a little better for just 'one' individual, that is a whole world of difference to that one and every thing we do is important. It would certainly do no good at all if we did not help that one for fear of not making a difference to the masses. Maybe Will's story can inspire others to take a stand for the welfare of those around them, whatever the odds.

I did not ever believe I would see Will again. I did not think he would ever escape the abuse from the previous home and everyone said it was a hopeless cause. Moreover, the chances of me being where he was if he ever escaped again were catastrophically minute. However, things came together to reunite us. We happened to be in the vet when the first call came through and we happened to drive by and see the door left open. So was this destiny? Or maybe where there is a Will, there most certainly is a way.

Postscript

Since writing Will's story, we sadly had to say goodbye to Storm, Patti and subsequent adopted greyhounds, Lady and Snow; and the cats: Humphrey, Molly and Winnie when their lives came to a close through illness or old age. We now have Oaky, Sylvie and Yogi the greyhounds, along with Bernard the rescued tortoise. Each of the greyhounds continue to exhibit the customary characteristics of the breed, but in their own unique and individual way. In each and with each is a new story and their own loving and uniquely bonded relationship with each other and with me.

Most devastatingly, after a long life and enjoying holidays and other animals coming into our lives, the pandemic hit and simultaneously Will was slowing down, having reached (we think), the age of thirteen years. I was so worried that we wouldn't be allowed to be with him if his legs went and we had to make a decision while Covid restrictions were in place. (I know many people suffered this isolation with loved ones, both human and animal) - it is such a significant moment to show that love at their end and when they need it at the most crucial time. Being with Will was imperative – how could I not be there at the end?

Restrictions started to ease and our vet was able to carry out procedures outside to enable people to be with their animals. They said how awful it was when people couldn't be there with them at the end. The dreaded day did come eventually, his legs gave way and the choice was taken away from us. There was nothing we could do, but let Will go with dignity and peace. We were allowed to be with him once a long-line had been set up to administer the required drugs. While we stood back as they inserted it as the pandemic restrictions required, I won't forget him turning to look for me. When we were allowed forward, we were able to hold him; and Will slipped away, his head in my arms, behind the big blue door leading into the yard of the vet.

All our loved ones stay with us forever, both in the love we share that remains, and as an intrinsic part of our own story. And Will will stay with me forever. I have requested my own body be placed with the ashes of my animals when we will all be together again.

Listening to the song, "The Waiting Room" by Lucy Spraggan (from album, "Today Was a Good Day") sets me off as it is an emotional look at the life of a beloved dog until the final goodbye in the vet. The lyrics seemed to be talking about Will. But the song is a lovely tribute to any loved animal.

Until we meet again.

If you can offer a home to an unwanted, abandoned or needy animal, please visit your local rehoming or rescue centre. Whittingham Kennels is one such charity which seeks to provide loving homes to retired and rescued greyhounds and other sighthounds. A donation will be made to for every book sold.

There are thousands of animals who just need a chance and a loving home. And the love you receive will be even greater than the love you give. Like Will's way.

Printed in Great Britain
by Amazon

23816605R00086